KEEPING PERSPECTIVE

Truths that Shape a
Life of Influence

Daniel Henderson

Keeping Perspective: Truths that Shape a Life of Influence
© 2010 by Daniel Henderson

Strategic Renewal
P.O. Box 365
Forest, VA 24551
strategicrenewal.com

Some of the anecdotal illustrations in this book are true to life and are included with the permission of the persons involved. All other illustrations are composites of real situations, and any resemblance to people living or dead is coincidental.

Unless otherwise identified, all Scripture quotations in this publication are taken from the HOLY BIBLE: The New King James Version (NKJV). Copyright © 1982 by Thomas Nelson, Inc. Used by permission. All rights reserved; the Holy Bible, New Living Translation (NLT), copyright © 1996, 2004. Used by permission of Tyndale House Publishers, Inc., Carol Stream, Illinois 60188. All rights reserved.

Scripture quotations are from The Holy Bible, English Standard Version® (ESV®), copyright © 2001 by Crossway, a publishing ministry of Good News Publishers. Used by permission. All rights reserved.

Scripture quotations marked (NASB) are taken from the New American Standard Bible®, Copyright © 1960, 1962, 1963, 1968, 1971, 1972, 1973, 1975, 1977, 1995 by The Lockman Foundation. Used by permission.

Scripture quotations marked (NIV) are taken from the Holy Bible, New International Version®, NIV®. Copyright © 1973, 1978, 1984 by Biblica, Inc.™ Used by permission of Zondervan. All rights reserved worldwide. www.zondervan.com

Scripture quotations marked (AMP) are taken from the Amplified Bible, Copyright © 1954, 1958, 1962, 1964, 1965, 1987 by The Lockman Foundation. Used by permission.

ISBN 978-0-9816090-1-0

Cover Design & layout by: Andrew Patterson
Cover Photo: Wojtek Kutyla

Contents

On Christian Living

On Prayer

Seasonal Thoughts

Introduction

For many years now, my father and pastor, Daniel Henderson, has been faithfully writing "e-devotionals" each week for his congregation. He has often told them "The hardest thing about the Christian life is that it is so daily." These short devotionals were meant to help them keep perspective, and encourage them in their daily life in Christ.

As a gift to my father, I began compiling the book you are holding now, a collection of the writings I have found to be the most helpful and encouraging in my own life. As I began working on this project, reading these devotionals over and over, I was deeply impacted as I realized the uniqueness of this book. To me, these are not chapters that flow out of some pastoral expertise. This is not another list of bright ideas to change the world. These are principles that I have seen lived out in my father's life – a life that he has by God's grace consistently modeled for my mother, my brother, my sister and I for many good and sometimes tough years. I am deeply grateful for this book, because it is the evidence of a faithful, dedicated husband and father. And ultimately, it is the evidence of a life lived passionately devoted to Christ and His Kingdom.

This book is not meant to be more spiritual fast food. It is meant to be a testimony of the sufficiency of God's grace in our daily experience as believers. As you read, I hope it will help you in some way, and the Lord will use it to encourage you as well.

D. Justin Henderson
January, 2010

On Christian Living

"The hardest thing about the Christian life is that it is so daily."

Trusting God When You are Trapped in Uncertainty

"Trust in Him at all times, you people; Pour out your heart before Him; God is a refuge for us."

Psalm 62:8

Recently I read a profound interchange documented in a book by the renowned ethicist John Kavanaugh[1]. He tells of when he went to Calcutta to work at "the house of the dying" for three months. This experience was part of his heartfelt search for personal direction. His first morning there, he met Mother Theresa. She asked him, "And what can I do for you?"

Kavanaugh asked her to pray for him. "What do you want me to pray for?" she asked him. He responded by explaining that he had come thousands of miles from the U.S. to find direction. "Pray that I have clarity," he told her.

She firmly responded to his request: "No, I will not do that." When he asked why, she said, "Clarity is the last thing you are clinging to and must let go of." Kavanaugh commented to her that she always seemed to have the clarity he longed for. She laughed and said, "I have never had clarity; what I have always had is trust. So I will pray that you trust God."

Our Clamor for Clarity

There is something in all of us that always wants clarity. It is part of our sinful ego, and perhaps a common expression of our insecurities. As illustrated in this exchange, clarity can become an idol that replaces real trust in God. In many ways, we would rather understand the details of the road ahead than become more intimate with the Builder of the road. Clarity can actually become spiritually counterproductive, as it shortchanges trust, a life of faith, and moment-by-moment dependence on God.

In the great "faith chapter," Hebrews 11, we are reminded that trust is strongest when life's circumstances are unclear. Noah built an ark for 120 years, waiting for an unprecedented rainfall. Sarah was told to trust God for a child in her old age, with no clarity as to how such a thing could happen. Abraham went out, not knowing where he was going, but planning to sacrifice his own son with no clarity as to what might occur, or why the stories are extensive, and the truth is unmistakable. Faith flourishes when we are trusting God through the unclear path of life.

Answers vs. Trust

So often we want to chart the course, but the Bible tells us to walk in the Spirit. We impose a strategic plan. Jesus says, "Follow me." We want all the answers. The Lord tells us to trust Him no matter what.

Recently, I discovered a song by a young Christian musician named Jadon Lavic[2]. The lyrics are precisely in tune with this biblical insight:

> You wake up to find
> That you're right where you're supposed to be
> Trapped in uncertainty
> Each day's a mystery
> You wake up to find
> That you're right where you're supposed to be
> The past is unveiled and you see
> You're right where you're meant to be

Friend, as you go through uncertain days, consider the truth we've been given. Faith, not certainty, is the single most important ingredient to a life pleasing to God.

Looking behind, we are familiar with His faithfulness and goodness, even when we did not perceive it at the time. He has not changed. You can trust him now. When we can't trace His hand, we can trust His heart. In the unpredictable seasons of life, may our hearts long not for clarity, but for faith.

A Genuine Belief

"So God created man in His own image; in the image of God He created him; male and female He created them."

Genesis 1:27

I recently attended a breakfast where Charles Colson was speaking. Not surprisingly, he spoke with dynamic eloquence on the importance of a biblical worldview and the urgency of embracing the sanctity of human life. Colson underscored the truth that because we are all created in the image of God, every human being should be treated with authentic and loving dignity.

The obvious application is that we value the sanctity of the unborn by opposing abortion and praying for women caught in the throes of this horrendous decision. We also dignify the sick and aging by providing respectful care until their divinely-ordered days on this earth expire. We honor the sanctity of human life by providing loving ministry, in Christ's name, to those in prison.

But why do we value human life? Why do we oppose abortion? Why pray for women caught in this tragic predicament? Is it a genuine belief in the sanctity of human life?

The foundation of our belief in the sanctity of human life is the truth that each human being is created in the image of God. It is an absurd contradiction to fight for the life of the unborn and still downgrade the life of an abortion doctor. A genuine belief in this truth must apply to every human relationship, not just some. It is not a selective truth. Even though we hate the sin, we must continue to love the sinner.

But consider the implications of applying this belief to only some and not others. One might argue that degrading the life of an abortion doctor is not necessarily denying the sanctity of his life, but only the loathing of his behavior. But do they not possess the image of God?

We desperately need to understand that the sanctity of human life is about more than just human life. It begins and ends with God. God created human beings in His image. Any assault on any human life, whether an unborn baby or an abortion doctor, is first and foremost an assault on God.

Still, it is often easier to verbally affirm a belief like this, as long as the application goes unchallenged. When it comes to honoring the life of the ugly, the despised, the shameful, the antagonistic, or the murderous, it's a tough order. If we allow ourselves selectivity in this area, we prove that our motivation is not because of a genuine and consistent belief in the sanctity of human life, but because of something else. The apostle John reminds us, "My little children, let us not love in word or in tongue, but in deed and in truth" (1 John 3:18). And I continually hear the Lord reminding me, "Do not honor the sanctity of human life and the dignity of every human soul just in word or in tongue – but in deed and in truth. And begin with the obvious."

Lord, help us to see people as you see them. They are created in your image, are in need of your love, and are deserving of dignity. I confess that I can only do this through the power of Jesus Christ.

A Kingdom Heart

"Your kingdom come. Your will be done..."
                                    Matthew 6:10

Based on the model for prayer Jesus gave us in Matthew 6:9-13, God's first concern for our lives is an intimate knowledge and understanding of His character, expressed in a life of worship and trust. "Our Father who art in Heaven, Hallowed be your name." This is the ultimate cry of an authentic life.

Likewise, I think it's true that the second great characteristic of an authentic life is a "kingdom heart." The next words to come out of Jesus' mouth were, "Your kingdom come, Your will be done on earth as it is in heaven." There is no way to fully elaborate here on the entire importance of these words, but explore with me in discovering some ways it applies to our lives today.

Rooted in spiritual reality, not religious form

We are familiar with the profound words in John 3:5-8, "Most assuredly, I say to you, unless one is born of water and the Spirit, he cannot enter the kingdom of God. That which is born of the flesh is flesh, and that which is born of the Spirit is spirit. Do not marvel that I said to you, 'You must be born again.'" The only way to experience and live out the kingdom is through the spiritual transformation of regeneration by the Spirit through the power of the Gospel.

The Kingdom of God is both internal and eternal. It is internal first, then manifested in it's exploits. In Luke 17:21 Jesus said, "For indeed, the kingdom of God is within you." The work of the kingdom is rooted in a fully submissive heart that prays for the rule of spiritual reality over all feeling, thought, action and life.

Just as the Pharisees in Jesus' day had become enamored with the forms of religion, sometimes we get caught in the activities and programs of Churchianity and neglect the real work of the Kingdom. This often includes the neglect of the Holy Spirit. Religious work flows from a religious heart. Kingdom work flows from a kingdom heart. There is a difference, not easily discerned, but very significant in the life of the true disciple.

Reflecting a Comprehensive Compassion

Jesus displays this compassion when He says, "Let the little children come to Me, and do not forbid them; for of such is the kingdom of God" (Mark 10:14). Just like the disciples, we often get so busy in our efforts to follow Christ that we forget His ever-large and always compassionate heart for people. It would be easy to conclude that one group is more important to the kingdom than another group, but this is false.

By honoring children, Jesus elevated the importance of childlike faith and an accepting heart. He also blew away the disciples' dispositions about who matters and who doesn't matter. We must entirely dispose of any human categories of value and significance.

Every person equally matters. Every heart matters. We need to daily remind ourselves that the lost souls in our community are important, and they need to be influenced not only through the declaration of the gospel, but also its demonstration.

Together, we must pray for a fresh revival across our land, compelling us toward a global impact in reaching the least, the last and the lost with the good news. That's a kingdom vision that can be cultivated within us. We long for kingdom hearts.

Never Satisfied with the Superficial

Paul wrote in Romans 14:17, "For the kingdom of God is not eating and drinking, but righteousness and peace and joy in the Holy Spirit." The Romans were concerned over meat offered to idols. Paul redirects them from their shallow vision to the things that count for the kingdom.

This truth is essential for all of us. A real kingdom heart is not preoccupied with style, method or personal preferences. Debates and divisions over the temporary and trivial are trumped by real kingdom concerns in the heart of the true disciple.

Longing for Inexplicable Impact

Paul wrote, "For the kingdom of God is not in word but in power" (1 Corinthians 4:20). Paul often confronted false teachers who took pride in their oratorical skill and force of personality. Paul exposed the lie that these human trappings were somehow relevant to real kingdom work. Paul also reminds us that the kingdom is about the power of God, which is contained in "earthen vessels" (2 Corinthians 4:7).

It has occurred to me that we can be "missional" without having a kingdom heart. We can be a praying people and not have a kingdom heart. We can sing, give, serve and sacrifice, all without a kingdom heart. Indeed, we cry out, "Your kingdom come, Your will be done." May God give us the grace to actually make this cry the guiding passion of all our feelings, thoughts and actions.

Beyond a Fickle Faith

"And let us not grow weary of doing good, for in due season we will reap, if we do not lose heart."

Galatians 6:9 (ESV)

One year during a Thanksgiving Eve service, our congregation took some time to hear spontaneous testimonies of God's work in the individual lives of the people. The stories were so encouraging, and we clearly needed it.

One such testimony was from Jean Smith. The essence of her gratitude was that she had crossed her 55th anniversary as a member of the church, and she wanted to give God all the glory for His working in her life over these years.

Trascending Feelings

Sadly, Jean is a stark contrast to what we commonly see today in the American church. I remember the wise words of an old mentor, Woody Phillips, Sr. He said with sadness, "Never forget that most people leave a church because it does not feel the same anymore." At the time, I thought it a strange comment. Now after 25 years as a pastor, I've concluded that Woody's wisdom was correct.

Emotions are important. God has certainly given them to us for a reason. We all face hurt, disappointment and setbacks that affect our feelings among any gathering of Christians. That is the nature of imperfect Christ-followers behaving in imperfect ways. The real issue is not if we have these feelings but what we do with them.

We are faced with a choice as Christians. We can fuel the negative emotions, and allow them to drive our decisions, or we can subject these feelings to real faith. When we subject them to real faith, the result is faithfulness to Christ, His church and His people.

Recently, I was reading *The Taste of Joy* by Calvin Miller. In the first chapter, he openly shares his own struggle with this issue: "In recent years I have learned the difference between faith and the moody obsession I once thought it to be. I once drove furiously to be happy, and in my confusion I called this mad urge the pilgrimage of faith. How slowly I learned that faith is not a hunger to be happy."

Miller continues: "So much sour Christianity has resulted from this happiness drive. It is often this compulsion which lures the frustrated to Christ for the first time. And the same drive continues in Christians as an insatiable appetite for ever higher and higher plateaus of mood."

Applying this idea to our church-attending habits, he says, "This damnable lust to titillate not only makes us miserable with what we have, it causes us to indict Christian worship. Most of us view church as an 'experience center,' where believers seek to 'feel' together in their pilgrimage. . . This glandular approach to joy assumes that God exists in his fullness to make Christians feel good. Church, however, does not exist to make us happy. . . While happiness may result from worship, joy is not the goal of great worship. Indeed it may precede it."

Here is the concern of every pastor. We long for our people to turn from the idol of "feeling" and to bow in persevering faith before the Holy One who is absolutely faithful in all of His character and dealings. This is spiritual maturity and health. And it is always good for the advancement of the kingdom.

Heroes of Faith Over Feeling

We must remember that our heroes of the faith did not always "feel good" about their calling, their relationships, or the non-support of other people. (Just review Hebrews chapter 11). I am sure Paul did not have much excitement about his constant rejection from the Jews. I doubt he felt good about being beaten and imprisoned for his message. His entire life of suffering, perseverance and faithfulness is a testament of the power of his words, "the just shall live by faith." Clearly, Jesus did not feel like leaving the glories of heaven to risk the vulnerability of humanity. He did not feel like confronting the Pharisaical hypocrisies of the religion of His day. He did not feel like being beaten, crucified and murdered. And we do not worship Him because He is the author and finisher of our feelings.

You are probably aware of the illustration that is often presented to a new convert. It depicts a train where the engine is "fact", the middle car is "faith," and the caboose is "feeling." We encourage new Christians to rest in the facts of God's Word and to live by a real and consistent faith. We tell them the caboose of feeling is incidental. It may come and go, but is not that basis of our Christian life.

Somehow, "established" Christians forget this. Maybe it is one of the devil's preferred deceptions. Somehow that caboose slips to the front of the train in our interactions and decisions. As expected, the result is a train wreck of our faithfulness, our friendships and our fruitfulness for Christ.

From my perception, Jean Smith has discovered the joy of enduring the good and the bad. She has remained steady under many imperfect church leaders. I am sure she's even had her feelings hurt a time or two. But no one will be calling her a "church hopper" anytime soon.

Don't Eat the Camels!

"Examine me, O Lord, and prove me; Try my mind and my heart."

Psalm 26:2

Imagine you are visiting your local zoo. As you approach the camel pen, you see a big sign: "Don't eat the camels!" You'd likely laugh at the sight.

Jesus posts just such a sign on the Christian pathway to spiritual maturity. It seems an odd warning. Jesus described the religious elite of His day as those "who strain out a gnat and swallow a camel" (Matthew 23:24).

His comment was a brief hyperbolic illustration in the context of the most scathing sermon of His earthly ministry. If you are feeling like you have thick skin today, you can read the entire message in Matthew 23:13-36. The common sermon title is "Eight Woes to the Religious Leaders."

He preached it among a large crowd in the temple as He pronounced his judgment on the Jewish religious elite. Some say it is in contrast to the eight blessings found in the Sermon on the Mount. Jesus the preacher didn't make any friends that day with this sermon.

The illustration is pointed at someone who takes great care to strain the small bugs out of their drinking water and then turns around to gulp down a camel without even realizing the contradiction and hypocrisy of the experience. It's like picking a speck of pepper out of food then eating a truck load of pepper plants. We might call it a very bad case of spiritual myopia, packed with contradiction, leading to destruction.

Camel Controversies

I once heard a firsthand report of a young pastor who recently called his church to pray and fast for the ministry, using Isaiah 58 as the foundation for the new endeavor. A few minutes later, three men disrupted their adult Bible class, arguing at the top of their lungs over the exact particulars of the passage.

I've known people who want to go "deep" into the scriptures and are entirely critical of any teacher whose delivery doesn't adequately meet their preferences. Yet, in their own lives they tolerate sinful habits and consistently exhibit a caustic and unrestrained tongue. I've also heard stories of church leaders who create significant disunity within the leadership team over an issue of personal preference. The examples are abundant. The "Hall of Shame for Christian Camel Eaters" is packed with ignoble examples.

As a pastor, I am responsible to encourage people to watch their dietary habits when it comes to gnats and camels. As one who has a burden for the body of Christ in our nation, I continually hope we can learn to stay away from the camels. So how do we avoid choking our personal, familial and congregational vitality through camel swallowing?

Myopia vs. Maturity

We must learn to discern. There is a difference between a selective approach of creating false standards of spirituality and then judging others by your preferential standard, and a truly Biblical approach. The only way to know the difference is to know the scripture enough to discern between myopia and maturity. Check your motives. Is your heart motivated by grace, coupled with a passion to edify others and build up the body? Or is your approach simply a desire to control others, and even the church?

Also, continually look in the mirror of Scripture. It's been said that the critic who begins with himself will have little time to take on outside contracts. Are you careful to evaluate your own heart, life and words first before launching your campaign against another brother or sister?

Learning to invite accountability is also critical. We often get so caught up in the subjectivity of our thoughts and feelings that we can't even see the camel we're feeding on. Ask a godly, discerning and courageous brother or sister to give you honest feedback about your behavior and words. Then, be ready to humbly listen and accept responsibility for whatever they tell you.

Likewise, it is imperative that you keep a clear conscience. If you find out you've been gulping camels and that you've hurt other believers or a group of believers, demonstrate the sincerity of your self-evaluation and repentance by confessing it to the Lord and humbly seeking the forgiveness of those you've hurt.

Live everyday with eternity in mind. All camel eaters will ultimately be exposed. Eternity is a long time to live with the regret of a camel diet. Let's keep Jesus' warning about hypocrisy and myopia in mind. Let it underscore your own desire for spiritual authenticity. Let it guide you into the heart of the gospel.

Faithful in Little Things, Fruitful in Big

*"Well done, good servant; because you were faith-
ful in a very little, have authority over ten cities."*

Luke 19:17

I've heard it said that when you do today what you have to do, the day
will come when you can do what you want to do. And I believe Jesus
established this principle with even greater clarity when he said, "He
who is faithful in a very little thing is faithful also in much" (Luke
16:10, NASB).

Scripture abounds with illustrations of this truth. I think of Joseph
who was faithful in his service to Potiphar, in spite of many setbacks,
and became second-in-command in Egypt. Moses was faithful to the
flocks of his father-in-law Jethro for 40 years before he became a great
deliverer of God's people. Joshua was a brave soldier and dedicated as-
sistant to Moses before he led the conquest of the Promised Land.

Furthermore, David was a faithful shepherd, protecting his father's
sheep from lions and bears, before God elevated him as King over
Israel. Nehemiah was a loyal cupbearer to a foreign ruler before God
summoned him to lead the effort to rebuild the wall of Jerusalem.
Matthias had faithfully followed Christ in the shadow of the "greater"
apostles for several years before the early church chose him to replace

Judas. The writer of Hebrews even speaks of our Lord Jesus describing Him as "Christ Jesus, who was faithful to Him who appointed Him" (Hebrews 3:1-2).

Jesus told the parable of the talents, commending the one who had been faithful with what he had been given: "Well done, good and faithful servant; you were faithful over a few things. I will make you ruler over many things. Enter into the joy of your lord." Of course, our ultimate reward is eternity with Christ, but it is encouraging to see him reward the faithful sacrifices of a diligent life by opening doors of greater responsibility and impact.

What about your journey? In a world of short-term and shaky commitments, do you trust Christ for the grace to endure hardship and misunderstanding and to remain faithful to your duties? Are you resolved to endure in your responsibilities after the entertainment is gone? In a world of unreliability, can you be counted on to remain faithful in and out of season? It is not always easy to keep your hand to the plow, but it is always worth it.

I am reminded that much of life seems mundane. It is important to let every occasion be a great occasion, for we never know when the Lord may be measuring us for a greater realm of influence. Be assured that our Lord sees and rewards it all. May you sense His pleasure today, and trust Him to greater measures as you serve Him faithfully.

I Have Decided to Follow Jesus...But Which One?

"If the world hates you, you know that it hated Me before it hated you."

John 15:18

Most of God's people love to sing. I am certainly one of them. As a child, I was raised on "the great hymns of the faith" which are full of theology and insight. During my teenage years, contemporary worship was just emerging, and I loved these new expressions of joy and spiritual passion. Music in many forms has shaped my spiritual journey and given rich expression to the desires and devotion of my heart.

One of the all-time classic songs of surrender is, "I Have Decided to Follow Jesus." But as I think of the hundreds of times I've sung this simple tune, I realize that the essence of the commitment it captures is not always apparent in my heart.

Like many, I sing songs about Jesus while imagining a Jesus that is made in my image; I picture a savior that is culturally acceptable, easy to follow and usually compliant with my worldview and my agenda.

I heard it said many years ago: "In the beginning God created man in His image. Ever since then man has been trying to return the favor." In Psalm 50:21, the Lord rebukes Israel for thinking that He was just like them. It is easy to concoct a Jesus in our modern stylized image, rather than capturing the reality of His heart and character. Our pledge to follow Him must be more than a pleasant tune and a mouthful of easy words.

The Fabric of Following

I often think about what it means to really follow Jesus. More than just the obvious dynamics of stepping out in faith and venturing into the "unknown," I find the Lord wanting me to understand the heart of Jesus and, by His grace, to make my heart the same. What do we really mean when we sing, "I have decided to follow Jesus?"

First, we must be willing to follow Jesus in His surrender. Philippians 2:5-9 speaks to us of Jesus' self-emptying. He surrendered His rights to His heavenly glory to serve the ultimate need of His creation. It says, "Let this mind be in you which was also in Christ Jesus who, being in the form of God, did not consider it robbery to be equal with God, but made Himself of no reputation, taking the form of a bondservant, and coming in the likeness of men. And being found in appearance as a man, He humbled Himself and became obedient to the point of death, even the death of the cross."

Even his agonizing cry in the garden echoed this resolve. He said, "Father, if it is Your will, take this cup away from Me; nevertheless not My will, but Yours, be done" (Luke 22:42). It seems that if we are really to follow Jesus, we must hold all things loosely, always ready, should He ask us, to surrender our possessions, positions or plans for the sake of serving others.

We must also be willing to follow Him in His sacrifice. John 10:11 reveals the heart of Jesus and His sacrifice: "I am the good shepherd. The good shepherd gives His life for the sheep." Again in John 15:13, we read, "Greater love has no one than this, than to lay down one's life for his friends." Costly faith has become somewhat of an oxymoron in our modern Christian culture. However, it should be standard faire for those who declare their desire to follow Jesus.

We must be willing to follow Jesus in his satisfaction as well. We all feel the pull to find satisfaction in our earnings, accomplishments, activities, family, friends and dreams for the future. But John 4:34 reminds us of what it would mean to follow in His steps. Jesus declared, "My food is to do the will of Him who sent Me, and to finish His work." The food, satisfaction and fuel of His existence were doing and completing the Father's will for His life. I am not a follower if I do not thrive on the same food that Christ desired. This is the only menu that comes with the promise of eternal satisfaction guaranteed.

And we must be willing to follow Jesus in His sensitivity. It is easy to live the Christian life on autopilot, doing our duties for the Lord but becoming too active to hear His voice of direction or redirection. Christ lived with a constant sensitivity to the will of the Father. "Most assuredly, I say to you, the Son can do nothing of Himself, but what He sees the Father do; for whatever He does, the Son also does in like manner" (John 5:19).

Following in the Moment

Further affirming this principle, Christ, said, "I can of Myself do nothing. As I hear, I judge; and My judgment is righteous, because I do not seek My own will but the will of the Father who sent Me" (John 5:30). If Jesus resolved to do nothing of Himself in order to respond moment by moment to the direction of the Father, I wonder how our path might be different if we committed to follow Him with the same approach.

I have decided to follow Jesus, as best as I know how in this moment of life. But when tomorrow comes, I cannot live on yesterday's resolve. My commitment must be fresh and new everyday; I must follow our Lord in a life of surrender, sacrifice, satisfaction and sensitivity.

God's Inventory

"But we have this treasure in earthen vessels, that the excellence of the power may be of God and not of us."

2 Corinthians 4:7

We all know that accomplishing certain jobs requires certain tools. A mechanic needs diagnostic automotive tools. Landscape workers need lawn mowers. Delivery companies need vehicles. Pastors need Bibles (even though many today never open one during a sermon). You get the idea.

In the most important task in the world (the redemption of humanity), the all-powerful Creator has restricted Himself to using people. He could have chosen perfect instruments or decided to use none at all. But by divine design, He uses flawed people.

We are described in 2 Corinthians as earthen vessels, unadorned clay pots, jars of clay. In biblical times these were very common (and often flawed) pots that were primarily used for household trash or carrying human waste. They were nothing special. Almighty God has chosen to restrict his work to tools like us.

Yet, the design is for His glory. He is so powerful, gracious, wise and sufficient that He can use this repertoire of imperfect, flaky, and unreliable human material to accomplish eternal work. What a God we serve. As you receive the truth of this Scripture, let Paul's words encourage you:

> *For you see your calling, brethren, that not many wise according to the flesh, not many mighty, not many noble, are called. But God has chosen the foolish things of the world to put to shame the wise, and God has chosen the weak things of the world to put to shame the things which are mighty; and the base things of the world and the things which are despised God has chosen, and the things which are not, to bring to nothing the things that are, that no flesh should glory in His presence. But of Him you are in Christ Jesus, who became for us wisdom from God — and righteousness and sanctification and redemption — that, as it is written, "He who glories, let him glory in the LORD"*
> *1 Corinthians 1:26-31*

Today, as you consider the amazing grace that has purchased your life at the cost of the blood of Christ, stand in awe. When you consider that with firm resolve and glorious purposes He has chosen to use your flawed humanity as the transmitter of His power, pour out your heart in humble gratitude. My fellow "jar of clay," join me in crying out with the Psalmist, "Not unto us, O LORD, not unto us, but to Your name give glory!" (Psalm 115:1).

Risk and Reward

"If then you were raised with Christ, seek those things which are above, where Christ is sitting at the right hand of God."

Colossians 3:1

In most endeavors of life, we regularly weigh the risk and the reward. Following Christ surely has its risks. Real discipleship can cost us our time, money, comfort, popularity and career advancement. It may even cost us our life.

Worth the Risk

It is never easy, often confusing and sometimes demanding beyond expectation. But it is always worth it. When you consider that lives are being changed for eternity, the so-called risk is really no risk at all.

At the end of his life, Paul declared the eternal perspective that kept him in the fight when the risks were painstaking and the rewards seemed elusive. He was hours away from having his life and ministry finished by Nero. Still he wrote, "Finally, there is laid up for me the crown of righteousness, which the Lord, the righteous Judge, will give to me on that Day, and not to me only but also to all who have loved His appearing" (2 Timothy 4:8).

Sometimes when we think of rewards and crowns, our concepts can be a bit ethereal. But Paul spoke very obviously about this in a few other passages too. Consider his words in Philippians 3:20-4:1: "For our citizenship is in heaven, from which we also eagerly wait for the Savior, the Lord Jesus Christ, who will transform our lowly body that it may be conformed to His glorious body, according to the working by which He is able even to subdue all things to Himself. Therefore, my beloved and longed-for brethren, my joy and crown, stand fast in the Lord, beloved."

Worthy Rewards

In light of Christ's reign and heaven's reward, Paul declared that the people to whom he ministered were his "joy and crown." Again, in 1 Thessalonians 2:19-20, Paul wrote, "For what is our hope, or joy, or crown of rejoicing? Is it not even you in the presence of our Lord Jesus Christ at His coming? For you are our glory and joy."

My joy and crown is not just in sermons I've preached, programs I've maintained or organizations I've established. The ultimate joy and crown will be the lives that have been changed in Christ, His word and His Spirit, through me. This is ultimately true for all of us.

What risks are you taking for Christ today? Do you believe, to the core of your being, that it is worth it? Will you focus on your eternal reward? Take time to list the joys and crowns of your life and ministry. Then, humbly thank our Lord Jesus Christ for the privilege of serving Him and, in some small way, being useful for His work in seeing lives transformed.

The Mystery and Power of Spiritual Momentum

"And let us not grow weary while doing good, for in due season we shall reap if we do not lose heart."

Galatians 6:9

I've been thinking lately of an intriguing concept called "spiritual momentum." Most of us are aware of the common theories about momentum in organizations. It has been called the "Big Mo" and is commonly known as a leader's best friend. The concept is huge in business and is often the key to winning a competitive athletic contest.

Of course, the Christian life and the work of the church are astoundingly different than a corporation or a football game. While Christian living and service is played out on the tangible field of earthly living, the source and nature of spiritual momentum can be very different. The criterion for spiritual momentum is not a statistical bottom line, but it is measured by eternal standards and in human hearts.

As best as I can understand it, spiritual momentum involves a deep enlivening of hearts that is rooted in a genuine work of the Spirit, is fueled by faith, and is ultimately evidenced in clear and Christ-honoring ways.

Spiritual momentum is different than natural momentum because it is often beyond our human senses of seeing, hearing and touching. It can even be in direct opposition to natural, numeric momentum. Paul described it this way: "Therefore we do not lose heart. Even though our outward man is perishing, yet the inward man is being renewed day by day. For our light affliction, which is but for a moment, is working for us a far more exceeding and eternal weight of glory, while we do not look at the things which are seen, but at the things which are not seen. For the things which are seen are temporary, but the things which are not seen are eternal" (2 Corinthians 4:16-18).

In a sense, Paul says, "outwardly momentum is waning but inwardly it is growing. The ultimate focus needs to be the spiritual and unseen because that is the momentum that is real and lasting."

There are times we try to generate and manipulate an external momentum in order to justify our existence or win the approval of people. Of course, there is value in some tangible "wins." We should always pray hard, work hard, strive for excellence and hope for the best in our lives and commitments, and then give God all the glory. But we must ultimately be attuned to the work of the Spirit throughout the "up" and "down" seasons of life.

Portrait of Momentum

We see this played out in many places in the Bible. Externally, the momentum was downward for Joseph during the years following his betrayal by his brothers. For many years he was in slavery and prison. He was misunderstood and maligned. Yet, a spiritual greatness was emerging in his life and finally came to fruition. He had the wisdom and grace to know that while man-made evil had externally inflicted him, God's goodness was constant, increasing and eventually prevalent in his life.

God reduced Gideon's army to a semblance of its former state, but spiritual momentum was growing, and ultimately resulted in a profound victory for the Lord's people. Judah was coming under attack in 2 Chronicles 20. King Jehoshaphat felt the "momentum" waning, but he cried out to the Lord in earnest, only to learn that God was growing a spiritual momentum in his midst that resulted in unusual and glorious victory. Jerusalem was broken down and without walls, but God was stirring a spiritual momentum in the heart of Nehemiah that eventually turned his prayers into progress and his burden into a rebuilding.

Applications of Momentum

In your own life, the momentum of your physical energy may be waning, yet the spiritual momentum of your impact may be at its highest level. Financially, you may be straining to make ends meet, but God is using this time to increase your faith and obedience like never before. Your career may have stalled in some way, but this is the time God is refining your motives and using your testimony to impact others. It is true in so many ways that man looks on the outward appearance, but God looks on the heart. It is the heart momentum that ultimately counts the most and lasts for eternity.

Ironically, individuals and churches can lose their spiritual momentum and not know it because their focus is on outward indicators that may or may not be accurate. Think of the churches in Revelation chapters 2–3. It appears they had some pretty good momentum in their teaching, activities and plans. The living Christ let them in on an important insight by telling several of them that their spiritual momentum had died a long time ago. One church even thought it was fully alive, but it was actually dead (Revelation. 3:1).

Calculating Momentum

So how do we cultivate spiritual momentum? God has given us the means of His grace in the word, prayer and living in the power of the Spirit, day by day. I truly believe as we do this, in ease and in pain – through the tangible victories and defeats – the all-important spiritual momentum of our lives will grow and eventually triumph. Real fruit will follow. This is the fruit that remains and is much more significant than any results we can generate in our flesh.

So next time you think about the momentum of your life, consider which measurement you want to use. While man-made momentum may result in monuments to human effort, spiritual faithfulness will produce enduring fruit that lasts. The choice is yours daily.

Weapons of Mass Distraction

"But Martha was distracted with much serving..."
Luke 10:40

One particular Sunday as I finished preaching at a wonderful church in Virginia, the senior pastor came to the pulpit to share his personal response to the message. He noted his ongoing battle with distraction in the ministry, citing it as a primary ploy of the devil in making Christian leaders ineffective. He described Satan's effort as being "Weapons of Mass Distraction." I've been pondering that statement, and I've concluded that the enemy does not have to destroy us, but simply distract us. Little distractions tolerated over a long period of time result in big disasters.

Twice in my ministry as a pastor, I have come to a mega-church in the wake of scandalous moral failure by my predecessor. The mass destruction is beyond imagination to the casual observer. But for the clean-up man who arrives next, the fallout is heartbreaking and long-lasting. Each of these disasters started with little distractions in the heart of good men. Fueled over time, the distractions led to spiritual disabilities. Eventually, those distractions became decisions that brought shame and reproach to the name of Christ.

The Best Choices

Yet, some of the most dangerous distractions are the "good" ones. They are tolerable, but they eventually ruin our trajectory in the journey of honoring Christ with a well-lived life. It is said so often that we almost become numb to its truth: "The good is usually the greatest enemy of the best."

I tell people often, "The power of 'no' is in a stronger 'yes'." The ability to discard distractions is rooted in a firm understanding of the best priorities. We must embrace these priorities with a passionate "yes" in our heart of hearts. When distractions come, "no" becomes a positive Christian word, because it is rooted in strong convictions about the best and highest commitments. I hold high my own conviction to help current and future leaders identify biblical priorities and then equip them to become confident and competent in implementing those priorities.

Choosing Your Yes's

These priorities are salient in the Scriptures. The familiar story of Martha and Mary comes to mind. Busy and distracted, Martha became frustrated and critical in the moment. Her sister Mary embraced a clear *yes* as she prioritized seeking Christ over serving Christ. Jesus commended her for her focus as being the *best* choice and the one that would ultimately matter in eternity (Luke 10:38-42).

I often preach on Acts 6:1-7. The early apostles refused to get distracted with the broken program for feeding the widows. They directed a process of finding qualified and godly servants to solve the problem, but they would not compromise their own commitment to "prayer and the ministry of the word." The result was that God blessed their focus with a powerful unleashing of His power. The word of God spread, the disciples multiplied greatly, and great numbers of hard-liner Jewish priests were miraculously converted. There was no such mass distraction among them.

Perhaps an even more powerful and clear reiteration of this principle is found in Exodus 18. Moses was overwhelmed and weary from judging the people. His astute father-in-law offered him some life-saving wisdom: "So Moses' father-in-law said to him, "The thing that you do is not good.

> *Both you and these people who are with you will surely*
> *wear yourselves out. For this thing is too much for you;*
> *you are not able to perform it by yourself. Listen now*
> *to my voice; I will give you counsel, and God will be*
> *with you: Stand before God for the people, so that you*
> *may bring the difficulties to God. And you shall teach*
> *them the statutes and the laws, and show them the way*
> *in which they must walk and the work they must do.*
> *Moreover you shall select from all the people able men,*
> *such as fear God, men of truth, hating covetousness;*
> *and place such over them to be rulers of thousands,*
> *rulers of hundreds, rulers of fifties, and rulers of tens.*
> *And let them judge the people at all times. Then it will*
> *be that every great matter they shall bring to you, but*
> *every small matter they themselves shall judge. So it*
> *will be easier for you, for they will bear the burden with*
> *you. If you do this thing, and God so commands you,*
> *then you will be able to endure, and all these people*
> *will also go to their place in peace"*
>
> *Exodus 18:13-23*

Jethro charged Moses with four essential priorities: pray (v. 19), teach the Word (v. 20), and train leaders and delegate important responsibilities to them. (vv. 21-22)

It is clear that this is a simple but profound defense against the devil's weapons of mass distraction. Yes! Yes! Yes! My friend, join me in asking God to deliver us from the ploy of the enemy to distract, discourage, disable and destroy our lives and ministries. The power of a focused life is like a laser-powered defense system against any weapon that is formed against us by the "master of distraction."

Predictability vs. Spirituality

"For all who are led by the Spirit of God are sons of God."

Romans 8:14 (ESV)

Why is it so difficult for churches to adapt to new approaches to ministry, even when these new activities are clearly biblical and fruitful for the sake of Christ's kingdom? This question has perplexed multiplied thousands of church leaders, and it is one I contemplated again recently in a conversation with a young man I am mentoring.

With a desire to bring a fresh work of prayer to his church, this young pastor in a small rural church changed the Sunday evening service from a teaching time to a worship–based prayer service. He did so with the full support of his church board. His heart was thrilled over the prospect of a fresh work of renewal in the hearts of the people. The prayer services seemed to be going well with fairly solid attendance.

A couple of months later, a few of the leaders asked him to discontinue the prayer times and return to the previous format. They said the people did not want to do it anymore. The pastor questioned the reasoning behind the opposition. The leaders simply said that they wanted to have a service they were used to. It was not that the service was not being well attended. They agreed that it was meaningful. They just wanted to keep things inside the box of another teaching service (although they already have two other teaching services during the week).

As the disappointed young leader and I talked about it, we concluded that these good church folks just wanted a predictable weekly worship routine and were content with the way things had always been.

Our Predictable Ruts

It occurred to me that this attitude of predictability is not, and cannot be, truly spiritual. In fact, in many ways, predictability is the polar opposite of spirituality.

When I speak of predictability, I am not minimizing the need for planning or orderliness. The Bible commands, "Let all things be done decently and in order" (1 Corinthians 14:40). Even our planning, however, needs to factor in flexibility. Proverbs 16:9 tells us, "A man's heart plans his way but the Lord directs his steps."

The predictability I speak of leaves little room for the Lord to truly direct the next step. Instead, it gives lip service to the Lord's real leadership, speaking of it but not wanting or allowing Him to change anything. Predictability locks in to a comfortable, mechanical approach to life and ministry that leaves little room for deviation, disruption, or change.

The Nature of Predictable Living

Three observations come to my mind as I think about the plight of predictability that tends to kill many needful, biblical, and spiritual initiatives.

Predictability is contrary to the character of the Holy Spirit

John 3:8 explains, "The wind blows where it wishes, and you hear the sound of it, but cannot tell where it comes from and where it goes. So is everyone who is born of the Spirit." The character and work of the Spirit is not predictable. Those who are born again ought to be fully surrendered to the Spirit, yielding their human need for a predictable life.

When Acts 2:2 described the coming of the Spirit at Pentecost, it says, "And suddenly there came a sound from heaven, as of a rushing mighty wind, and it filled the whole house where they were sitting." This unscripted coming of the Spirit initiated the reality of the church that day. The entire book is best described as "The Acts of the Holy Spirit," and is void of anything too predictable.

Romans 8:14 reminds us, "For as many as are led by the Spirit of God, these are sons of God." Too many believers have settled into a predictable system of religion rather than an expectant, flexible, and biblical spirit of submission to the real leadership of the Holy Spirit in their lives, homes, and churches. The Christian life is an adventure in the Spirit, wherein our security is not found in the status quo traditions of Christian activity, but in the joy of living in obedience to the Kingdom-oriented call of our living, creative, and all-sufficient Lord.

Predictability is contrary to the exercise of faith

Hebrews 11:1 offers this powerful definition: "Now faith is the substance of things hoped for, the evidence of things not seen." There's not much that is very predictable about that description. In fact, Hebrews 11 is full of examples of "heroes of faith" who lived unpredictable lives for God's glory. At the end of the chapter, this spirit of unpredictable obedience is captured in these words: "They wandered in deserts and mountains, in dens and caves of the earth" (Hebrews 11:38). Admittedly, that is not what most of us had in mind when we obeyed the salvation call to follow Christ – but it does speak of the need for a flexible, open-handed, and open-hearted readiness to walk in the Spirit anytime, anywhere, and in any way.

Predictability is contrary to the advancement of Christ's Kingdom

If we take time to consider the lifestyle, yieldedness, and journeys of the great people of God in biblical and church history, we will find the common denominator of many unpredictable tests and turns that shaped them into real world-changers. Christ's Kingdom advances very often, and most powerfully, in an environment of surrender to the immediate but trustworthy leadership of the Spirit.

A Call to Vibrant Spirituality

"We've never done it that way before" is not a complaint heard from the lips of those who understand the leadership of the Spirit, the nature of faith, and the priority of the Kingdom of Christ. "Here am I, Lord, send me" is the cry of a trusting, Spirit-sensitive heart. May the latter be the daily default drive of our hearts and lives.

A.W. Tozer wrote that the essence of true Christianity is "spontaneity, the sovereign moving of the Holy Spirit upon and in the free spirit of redeemed men. This has through the years of human history been the hallmark of spiritual excellence, the evidence of reality in a world of unreality."[3] He goes on to note that when our faith "loses its sovereign character and becomes mere form, this spontaneity is lost also, and in its place come precedence, propriety, system...the belief that spirituality can be organized...numbers, statistics, the law of averages, and other such natural human things. And creeping death always follows... Nothing but an internal spiritual revolution can deliver the victim from his fate." ("Beware the File Card Mentality" from the book *Of God and Men*.)

My prayer today is this: *"Oh God, give this revolution to the congregation my young friend leads. Give it to me each day. Give it to all of us as we continue in the unpredictable adventure of following Christ."*

The Measure of Your Success

"...the fire will test each one's work, of what sort it is."

1 Corinthians 3:13

Do you feel successful in life? If so, why? If not, why not? What is the measure of your evaluation?

Sadly, many evaluate success by false standards or subjective feelings. Neither is a true measure. The external, materialistic measures of this world are ultimately temporal and meaningless. King Nebuchadnezzar (Daniel 4:28-37) paraded the success of his skill, position, and wealth, only to face the fragility and emptiness of this approach. He is but one of countless examples of those who achieved and accumulated, only to still find a huge hole in the soul, overwhelmed with confusion and dissatisfaction.

Likewise, our self-assessments of success are often very limited and short-sighted. Like Mr. Holland in the film Mr. Holland's Opus, who felt very insignificant until he suddenly realized the amazing impact of his life, we, too, can lose sight of the real goal among the fog of the daily grind.

I heard a definition of success many years ago that I have never forgotten: "Success is when the people who know you best respect you the most." While we can't measure this ideal of success, we certainly can embrace and pursue it for our gain, others' good, and God's glory.

The Right Definition

Why is this definition important? I see several reasons. This kind of success values *people over productivity*. Those who neglect or disregard people in their hot pursuit of the almighty dollar, the bigger organization, or the next prominent title really lose in the contest of life. They have traded temporal things in exchange for the eternal value of souls. Jesus reminds us that, like Him, we are not here to be served (in pursuit of personal ambitions) but to serve and give our lives away for the needs of others – especially those who know us the best. When our quest for the goal leaves a wake of wounded souls and broken hearts, we have lived a very misguided life.

This definition elevates *integrity over impressiveness*. We all know the allure of living an impressive life where the crowds, the customers, and the clients all sing our praises. But the despair of knowing that the real substance of our life is unraveling behind the scenes is tormenting. I think the proper balance is found in the familiar quote, "If it doesn't work at home, don't export it." Success starts at the core of who we are, the people to whom we relate most closely, and the life we conduct when the crowds are not tracking us.

Most importantly, this kind of success elevates God's glory over ours. In our own fleshly talent, personality, and determination, we can all "succeed" at a lot of things. Only Christ, by His grace and indwelling power, can shape a life of highly respected and truly genuine character. As Jesus said, "Abide in Me, and I in you. As the branch cannot bear fruit of itself, unless it abides in the vine, neither can you, unless you abide in Me. I am the vine, you are the branches. He who abides in Me, and I in him, bears much fruit; for without Me you can do nothing... By this My Father is glorified, that you bear much fruit; so you will be My disciples." (John 15:4, 5, 8)

Living Toward Real Success

How do we progressively journey toward this destination of success? First, we must live in daily spiritual reality. The inner part of ourselves must be renewed day-by-day so that we do not conform to the values and visions fed to us by a superficial society. Instead, we must live out of a transformed "core "developed each day from glory to glory in the reality of His presence and Word.

Second, we must live with regular relational conscientiousness. We've heard the wise advice about keeping short accounts. We do this by regular, self-honest confession of our sins and failures toward God (1 John 1:9). We also must do it by making sure that we address all offenses on our part and any harbored bitterness toward others with the daily resolve of a clear conscience. Paul said in Acts 24:16, "I myself always strive to have a conscience without offense toward God and men." Jesus warned against our tendency to go through the motions of a religious life without a radical commitment to valuing authentic relationships (Matthew 5:24). When we fail to do this, not only are we miserable inside, but we lose our respect in rapid fashion. I learned a long time ago that my kids did not expect me to be perfect; they just needed me to be honest and make things right when I was wrong.

Also, we must live with Spirit-controlled consistency. Really, a life where those who "know us best respect us the most" can only occur under the moment-by-moment control of the Spirit of Christ. He produces the fruit of a respectable life in us (Galatians 5:22-25). The portrait of a successful life is painted from the palette of the Spirit's love, joy, peace, longsuffering, kindness, goodness, faithfulness, gentleness and self-control. Left to ourselves, we are all disrespectable jerks. Under His control, we can be an immense blessing to others – especially the ones who know us best.

So, here's to your success. May it be real and rewarding for you and the ones who love you –and want to help you succeed.

Tailor-Made Grace

"But he said to me, 'My grace is sufficient for you,
for my power is made perfect in weakness.'
Therefore I will boast all the more gladly of my
weaknesses, so that the power of Christ may rest
upon me."

2 Corinthians 12:9 (ESV)

Perhaps we've become so accustomed to the classic hymn that we have
forgotten how amazing grace really is. One of the truths about grace
that consistently fascinates me is that "God has tailor-made grace for
everything we face."

Most of us don't have too many tailor-made belongings. Some of us
have suits, shoes, draperies, and assorted possessions that have been
specially designed for their unique tastes. For the rest of us, I think of
the illustration of Extreme Makeover: Home Edition, which demonstrates the marvel of tailor-made blessings. In this broadcast, a needy
family, without their own capability, receives a brand-new home from
the riches of the television program and its sponsors. Everything is
suited to their longings – from the layout of the house and the style
of the furniture to the color of the paint and the décor of every room.
They even receive an abundance of mind-blowing extras.

That is a picture of tailor-made grace. Paul learned that Christ's grace
was sufficient for him in every way (2 Corinthians 12:9-10). Peter
describes God's grace as "manifold," which means it is diverse, multi-
faceted, and measureless in its variations.

I want to share with you three principles that help us grasp the wonder of tailor-made grace:

To experience grace, I must expect it!

John 1:16 says that out of Christ's abundance we have all received "grace upon grace." Or, as the Amplified Version (AMP) elaborated, "We were all supplied with one grace after another and spiritual blessing upon spiritual blessing and even favor upon favor and gift heaped upon gift." That is a lot of potential and powerful grace that we should expect from our Lord's abundant supply.

Just as we expected and experienced sufficient, transforming grace and power when we came to Christ, so we should live each day with confident expectation that His provision will be enough. Grace is not just a past-tense salvation miracle; it is a present-tense sanctification miracle. Do you live each day expecting His fresh miracles of grace in your life?

To recognize grace, I must understand it!

I like to define grace as "God doing for me, in me and through me what only He can do, through the person and power of Jesus Christ." This grace is not a crutch for the lazy or irresponsible. Grace works in conjunction with my grace-empowered efforts, not instead of them. Paul wrote of this when he said, "But by the grace of God I am what I am, and His grace toward me was not in vain; but I labored more abundantly than they all, yet not I, but the grace of God which was with me" (1 Corinthians 15:10).

Grace and laziness are incompatible. Grace is not about some "let go and let God" passivity on our part. But grace meets us in order to do what we cannot do. Still, everything we do is but an overflow of constant provisions of His grace. It may sound like a riddle, but it is a powerful truth with which to grapple.

Biblical grace works to make me like Jesus, not to make life easier. Grace is not an escape to some leisurely world where life is safe, pressures disappear, and all is flowers and fun. Grace is an escape from the devastating powers of this world's allures and deceptions. As Titus 2:11-12 says, "For the grace of God that brings salvation has appeared to all men, teaching us that, denying ungodliness and worldly lusts, we should live soberly, righteously, and godly in the present age." Do you want to see someone who understands grace? Look for the fruit of Titus 2:11-12 in his or her life.

Grace works for God's glory, not mine. Ephesians 2:7-9 reminds us that He is lavishing grace upon us in order to demonstrate the exceeding riches of His grace, for His own glory. None of this is of our "works," lest any person should boast.

To maximize grace, I must embrace weakness!

Jesus taught Paul, "My strength is made perfect in weakness." Paul learned this lesson so powerfully that he proclaimed, "Most gladly I will rather boast in my infirmities, that the power of Christ may rest upon me...for when I am weak, then I am strong" (2 Corinthians 12:9-11).

Paul learned and wanted us to grasp the truth that grace and self-sufficiency are incompatible. He also came to understand that weakness is not a circumstance; it is a choice!

His thorn in the flesh started as a circumstance that drove him to the throne of grace, but it became a choice that allowed him to constantly derive all that he needed from that source. He boasted of his weakness and made it a deliberate choice over and over again, because he knew this was the doorway to grace (see 1 Corinthians 2:3-5; 2 Corinthians 3:5, 11:30, 12:5, 13:4, 13:9).

Again, all of this grace is tailor-made. As a pastor for more than two decades, I've witnessed amazing displays of saving grace, suffering grace, guiding grace, sustaining grace, unifying grace, dying grace, and a multitude of other beautiful manifestations of His undeserved grace.

I like to think of grace as an "I.V." to the heart, flowing with unique and moment–by–moment formulas of Christ's provision. Just like a patient receives an instantly delivered formula of sustenance, so do we in Christ. Just as in the physical realm, that formula can be supplemented with a myriad of antibiotics, pain medications, blood thinners, anti-inflammatory aids, and other drugs –so the Lord does provide exactly what we need, how we need it, and when we need it. It really is amazing, isn't it?

Authenticity Through Accountability

"A man who isolates himself seeks his own desire;
He rages against all wise judgment."

Proverbs 18:1

Poet and preacher John Donne wrote, "No man is an island, entire
of itself...."[4] This is especially true of Christ followers and accents a
necessary practice of those who have been baptized together by the
Spirit into one body. In fact, we are an integral part of one another as
believers. We need each other for the sake of encouragement, mutual
ministry, fulfillment of our shared mission, and personal character
development.

The Source of Authenticity

The willingness to be genuinely connected and accountable cannot be
reduced to a legalistic series of discomforting questions or a written
report to a heavy-handed spiritual advisor. Real accountability springs
from the willingness of the heart to be in biblical relationship with
other believers. It is the fruit of a deep passion to live an authentic
life. "Getting by" is not acceptable for the one who desires accountability. An accountable Christian knows that while he cannot fool God, he
can fool others —but he chooses to do neither.

In a recent Strategic Renewal staff meeting, a team member was commenting on Galatians 2:1–10. We began to realize that there was in these verses a powerful example of accountability birthed from a passion for authenticity, as seen in the approach of Paul, the apostle. A portion of the passage says:

> *"Then after fourteen years I went up again to Jerusa-*
> *lem with Barnabas, and also took Titus with me. And I*
> *went up by revelation, and communicated to them that*
> *gospel which I preach among the Gentiles, but privately*
> *to those who were of reputation, lest by any means I*
> *might run, or had run, in vain... and when James,*
> *Cephas, and John, who seemed to be pillars, perceived*
> *the grace that had been given to me, they gave me and*
> *Barnabas the right hand of fellowship, that we should*
> *go to the Gentiles and they to the circumcised."*

Of course, I encourage you to read this section on your own, but here are some profound observations that might help you to desire a genuine and healthy sense of accountability in your life:

• Paul was an apostle called and commissioned directly by Christ who was willing to take the initiative to submit his ministry to the spiritual leaders in Jerusalem for consultation and accountability. He did not let his position of authority or his own experience of spiritual power prevent him from pursuing a submissive approach to life and ministry.
• Paul was well entrenched in his own effective and powerful ministry for about 14 years, but he was still willing to confer with others for evaluation. He stayed open to the teaching of others even when he was already "successful" in his own right.
• Paul refused to be a lone ranger. Even in going to Jerusalem, he took Barnabas and Titus with him. It was his custom to surround himself with other godly associates everywhere he went.
• Paul also recognized the importance of mutual accountability as he was forced to confront the powerful apostle Peter on

a later occasion (see vv. 11-21) over a serious breach of truth and uprightness. Even this is an expression of an authentic love for Christ and His truth. Paul knew, as we do, that accountability can be risky. We must be willing to lose our own standing in the eyes of others in order to help them embrace truth.

Much more could be said about this passage, but the bottom line is this: If the great Apostle Paul willingly pursued accountability for how he lived and what he taught, shouldn't we constantly seek to grow in our own character through a humble, consistent, and genuine accountability to others?

Pursuing an Accountable Life

Over the years in my own life, I have realized my own need for this. For more than two decades as a senior pastor, I met every week with the chairman of the elders at my church for spiritual accountability and mutual encouragement. I needed it, and we both benefited. Even now, in more of a "parachurch" ministry, I meet weekly with a spiritual mentor, gather with a group of men for Bible study, and seek to keep my life as an open book before my wife, family, and co-workers.

I have learned that accountability is not a system but an approach to life and relationships that values transparency, consistency, and mutual submission. Because I know my own weakness and pride despite my desire to live an authentic life, I must pursue accountability regularly – and for a lifetime.

By way of application, consider these questions that might help us all move toward a more genuine accountability for the sake of our authenticity:

1. Am I willing to submit my personality, approach, accomplishments, and plans to other godly believers without reacting in pride and defensiveness? If not, why not?

2. Am I willing to get into a regular covenant relationship with

other believers who will care for me, be honest with me, and
help me in my spiritual journey? If not, why not? If so, when
will I start and what will it look like?

3. Who do I know that could give honest feedback without fear
of reprisal or reaction from me? Can I contact them this week?
Can I get into a routine of honest, transparent communication
with another believer about my life, my struggles, my attitudes, my relationships, and my plans for the future?

4. If I do not do this, what consequences might occur? If I do
take this step, what blessings might I expect?

Proverbs 18:1-2 says, "A man who isolates himself seeks his own
desire; he rages against all wise judgment. A fool has no delight in
understanding, but in expressing his own heart." We have all felt the
temptation to withdraw from those who tell us the things we need
to hear but do not like to hear. Yet staying the course and pursuing
truth-telling relationships is the key to understanding – and ultimately, an authentic life.

The Eternal Scoreboard

"Not everyone who says to me, 'Lord, Lord,' will enter the kingdom of heaven, but the one who does the will of my Father who is in heaven."

Matthew 7:21 (ESV)

One of my most frequent "Danielisms" (as my friends call them) is the saying: "The scoreboard is in heaven." I guess this is my own version of the familiar adage, "Only one life, twill soon be past. Only what's done for Christ will last."

Yet in my mind, good theology requires that we take this idea a step further. Not everything "done for Christ" will actually last. The heavenly scoreboard and Sovereign Scorekeeper are profoundly and divinely discriminating.

Remember Matthew 7:21-23. The haunting passage reads, "Not everyone who says to Me, 'Lord, Lord,' shall enter the kingdom of heaven, but he who does the will of My Father in heaven. Many will say to Me in that day, 'Lord, Lord, have we not prophesied in Your name, cast out demons in Your name, and done many wonders in Your name?' And then I will declare to them, 'I never knew you; depart from Me, you who practice lawlessness!'"

That is an astounding and frightening declaration from Jesus Christ, the one by whom God will judge the secrets of every heart (Romans

2:16). Clearly it is not just the things "done for Christ" that last. There is something more. If we are going to understand the real score of life, there are essential truths we must affirm. To do so, let's examine three basic questions:

> 1. What is the difference between the earthly and eternal scoreboards?
> 2. What makes the difference on the eternal scoreboard?
> 3. Why does it matter?

What is the Difference?

Probably the best passage to describe the difference between the two scoreboards is Matthew 16:24-27, which reads, "Then Jesus said to His disciples, 'If anyone desires to come after Me, let him deny himself, and take up his cross, and follow Me. For whoever desires to save his life will lose it, but whoever loses his life for My sake will find it. For what profit is it to a man if he gains the whole world, and loses his own soul? Or what will a man give in exchange for his soul? For the Son of Man will come in the glory of His Father with His angels, and then He will reward each according to his works.'"

Clearly, the earthly scoreboard is tabulated by the things we do to hang on to the temporal definitions of this life. The cultural icon of the earthly scoreboard is the lifestyles of the rich and famous. Eternity will not reward or recognize what we have done out of a love for this world and things thereof. Net worth and superficial definitions of self-worth do not translate into eternal worth.

On the other hand, Jesus says that eternity will reward those things done in loving sacrifice for Christ, His glory and His kingdom. These grace-empowered deeds focus on "things that are not seen" rather than the things that are tangible and measurable. "For the things which are seen are temporary, but the things which are not seen are eternal" (2 Corinthians 4:18).

I often speak of the wealthy Christian executive who kept a plaque on his desk in his penthouse office that read, "It's all going to burn." Everything we see with our eyes is going to burn, rot, rust or go to the dump. All the tangible bells and whistles of the earthly scoreboard will disappear into irrelevance in light of eternity.

What Makes the Difference?

Putting this discussion into a strictly Christian context, how do we know what really registers on eternity's reward board for a believer? The Bible teaches that not all Christian activity is rewarded. In summary, I have come to believe that it is not just what we do – but how we do it, why we do it, and for whom we do it. It is not just enough to want to do things that matter in eternity. It is imperative that we conduct our lives in the right way, for the right reason, and for the Lord's glory, not our own.

So, how do we do this? First, Paul gives this defining piece of wisdom: "Now if anyone builds on this foundation (Jesus Christ) with gold, silver, precious stones, wood, hay, straw, each one's work will become clear; for the Day will declare it, because it will be revealed by fire; and the fire will test each one's work, of what sort it is. If anyone's work which he has built on it endures, he will receive a reward. If anyone's work is burned, he will suffer loss; but he himself will be saved, yet so as through fire" (1 Corinthians 3:12-15).

Again, the assumption is that everyone in this passage is building on the foundation of Jesus Christ – living for the Gospel and working for eternity. But the sort of work, the nature of it, and the character of it will be evaluated by the fire of eternal evaluation. Am I doing eternity's work in an un-Christlike fashion, or an injurious way, or with moral compromise? If so, it will ultimately be proven to be merely wood, hay, and straw.

Second, I must ask the "why?" question. This is the issue of my true motive. I can do all the right things for all the wrong reasons. Jesus warned in Matthew 6:1-17 that the external acts of fasting, praying and giving can be done with an impure motive that undermines any eternal recognition of the religious act. Even in diligent service for Christ we must constantly invite the God of truth and the truth of God to expose our motives in the presence of the One to Whom we must all give an account (Hebrews 4:12-13).

Third, I must constantly and prayerfully evaluate the one for whom I am doing what I am doing. The Psalmist declares in Psalm 115:1, "Not unto us, O LORD, not unto us, but to Your name give glory." This must be our cry, because we serve a God who declares, "My glory I will not give to another" (Isaiah 42:8).

These matters are hard to define because our own hearts can deceive us. The real nature of our motives can elude us. We can easily justify fleshly methodologies because we are implementing them "in His name." We can mask a self-glorifying accomplishment with a tacked-on "Praise the Lord." But someday, the infallible scoreboard will register the truth about what we've done. All other opinions and voices will be silenced. The score will stand, forever.

Why Does it Matter?

So, why does it even matter? On this side of eternity it matters because we cannot just live the Christian life and conduct Christian service on spiritual autopilot. Not all that we see and experience in our modern-day Christian culture is going to make the grade of the eternal evaluation. Not everything that is big, impressive, reported in Christian magazines, and blessed with "results" is going to register in heaven.

This is not a call to some kind of morbid introspection that immobilizes your spiritual impact. It is, however, a serious call to pure, Christ-honoring, loving and thoughtful service that not only targets eternity but also honors eternity's values here on earth.

Ultimately, it matters because whatever is on our scoreboard in heaven will be directly linked to our capacity to give Christ glory in eternity. Our crowns will all be cast at His feet (Revelation 4:10). Jesus tells us in Matthew 20:16, The first shall be last and the last shall be first. I believe millions of unknown Christians, in all kinds of vocations and locations, who serve their beloved Savior in pure and passionate ways, will have a great capacity to glorify Jesus in eternity. Likewise, I believe many "renowned" Christian leaders, touting grand exploits for Jesus, will be surprisingly empty-handed on that day.

I am certainly not the judge of the final evaluation around the throne. But I do need to judge my own heart everyday regarding what I do, how I do it, why I do it, and for whom I do it. These concerns must regulate all of my life and service – because the only scoreboard that matters is in heaven.

The Value of Suffering in Relationships

"The fruit of the Spirit is...longsuffering,"
Galations 5:22

Many years ago, I sat with a friend and highly respected marriage counselor. As he spoke about the many couples he had worked with over the years, he made a statement I will never forget. He said, "The problem with American Christianity is that we have no theology of suffering."

Many marriages and friendships end because one or both parties are unwilling to endure suffering. In our self-centered, consumer-driven culture, we tend to view relationships like a convenience store, which exist to meet our needs and improve our lot in life.

From a biblical standpoint, relationships are indeed vital to a wholesome existence and the fulfillment of God's purposes for our lives. However, they are also one of God's primary character development tools. Over the long haul, relationships bring incredible joy – but they can also be an avenue of necessary suffering. Both sides of the coin are essential.

One of the keys to healthy, enduring relationships is the quality of "longsuffering." This biblical idea is not popular in today's world, as we tend to turn away from anything that involves intentional pain. Yet the power of this quality in our lives is profound and essential in every lasting relationship.

Definition and Source

The original Hebrew word for longsuffering means "long of breathing" and is the opposite of anger ("short of breathing" or "violent breathing"). In the New Testament, the idea involves a person who is "long of soul" and indicates bearing long with people. One definition I like defines the word as "refusing to give up hope in a relationship." One synonym for longsuffering is "fortitude".

It is often translated "patience." Of the two Greek words used for "patience" in the New Testament, one refers to patience with people and the other speaks of patience with circumstances. Longsuffering is the first term and is vital in dealing with others.

God is the author and ultimate example of longsuffering. Numbers 14:18 states, "The LORD is longsuffering and abundant in mercy, forgiving iniquity and transgression." Psalm 86:15 affirms, "But You, O Lord, are a God full of compassion, and gracious, longsuffering and abundant in mercy and truth."

Of course, God is the source of our ability to experience and express longsuffering. Our very salvation is an expression of His longsuffering. Romans 2:4 tells us, "Or do you despise the riches of His goodness, forbearance, and longsuffering, not knowing that the goodness of God leads you to repentance?" His longsuffering heart towards us motivates us to repent and pursue intimacy with such a wonderful God.

As believers, we can expect that His Spirit in us will manifest longsuffering. Galatians 5:22 tells us that one of the fruit of the Spirit is longsuffering. Colossians 1:11 promises that God will strengthen us "with all might, according to His glorious power, for all patience and longsuffering with joy." When friends get on our nerves, children let us down, spouses become difficult, and work associates stab us in the back for the tenth time – His longsuffering heart can control our attitudes and actions if we yield to His power.

Four Keys to Practicing Longsuffering

In considering the value and practice of longsuffering, here are four specific points of advice:

Refuse to give up positive hope

As long as God's character of longsuffering does not change (and it never will) and as long as His Spirit lives in our hearts (and we are "sealed" in this assurance), we can believe that God is able to impart all we need for the positive progress of a relationship. He is able to change hearts and lives. We should always let Him start with our own– then trust Him to do the same for others.

Resolve to speak helpful truth

In his book *The Last Lecture*, author Randy Pausch states, "When you're messing up and no one says anything to you that means they've given up on you." A longsuffering heart is willing to "speak the truth in love" even when it involves temporarily risking one's standing with that person. This enduring commitment to the highest good of another person compels us to give him or her helpful, honest input even when it hurts. To do otherwise is to give up on that person. A longsuffering person doesn't make that choice.

Resist giving in to negative emotion

It's been said, "Emotions have no brains." Longsuffering is violated when we allow our emotions to rush beyond the controlling power of the Holy Spirit. Our thoughts become irrational and our words unloving. We react in ways that we later regret. As the definition suggests, longsuffering involves being "long of breath," which implies a steady, measured response as compared to a hotheaded impulse.

Remember character over convenience

Relationships are not a disposable convenience. They are a gift from God that must be treasured and embraced, even when it seems difficult and painful. A convenient life is seldom a life of deep character. It is in the fire that we are refined and made strong. Sometimes this refinement involves a demanding marriage, a rebellious child, an unreasonable boss, or a less-than-perfect fellow Christian. These relationships may not be easy – but they are worth it, because God uses them to make us more like Jesus.

English historian and novelist Arthur Helps said, "Strength is born in the deep silence of long-suffering hearts; not amid joy."[5] Mother Theresa offered these encouraging words: "Patient endurance attaineth to all things; who God possesseth in nothing is wanting; alone God sufficeth."[6] We all love the joyful highs that come with our relationships. This, too, is a gift from God. But if you are in the midst of a hard time in a relationship, be assured that God is pouring strength into your soul and that He will be sufficient in this season – as you learn the value of Christ-honoring and Christ-empowered longsuffering.

Our New Normal

"Set your mind on things above, not on things on the earth."

Colossians 3:2

Watchman Nee believed that most of us live such a subnormal Christian life that when a person lives a normal Christian life, we think they are abnormal[7]. If this was true when Nee penned it decades ago, it certainly seems relevant today.

Many times we become accustomed to the usual and dismal state of affairs in Christianity. It is easy to allow the standard of the less committed to become our standard. It is much easier to become content in our apathy.

Sometimes, before we know it, the materialism of our neighbor begins to dominate and dilute our own convictions. Or maybe the spiritual timidity of our circle of friends becomes our barometer for evangelism. We begin to compromise ourselves, and even our very souls. The devil is a specialist at blinding the minds of people. He is always delighted to blur our view of the gospel.

Our Source for a New Normal

In every area, our lives are to be based on the constancy and sufficiency of the Holy Spirit, never the declining pattern of spirituality around us. The work of the Holy Spirit is to make us more and more like Christ, not our culture.

I was recently reflecting on the many moments of failure among the disciples prior to Pentecost (even though they had the Perfect Teacher). They lacked insight, did not understand the person and plan of Christ, and eventually denied and deserted their Lord.

But after Pentecost, these followers were permanently indwelt and empowered by the Holy Spirit. This was a first in Biblical history. The abiding and indwelling Spirit transformed these flakey followers into powerful change-agents with a new capability and a very clear standard.

A Snapshot of a New Normal

In reflecting on this, I concluded several things about the Biblical "normal" vs. our cultural comfort level of spiritual experience. The normal Christian life should include the following:

- An ability to experience clear understanding and application of truth
- A lifestyle of spiritual refreshment
- A life of courageous witness
- A deep and insightful prayer life
- A powerful unity among believers
- A consistent demonstration of the character of Christ

It is encouraging to know that with a vision to transform the world through the power of the Gospel of Jesus Christ, for His glory, we are clearly empowered for this cause. It can happen. It must happen. But it must first happen in us if it is to occur through us.

Lord, help us to want what we ought to want. Increase our desire for your Holy Spirit. Reveal with clarity your standards, and let our hearts take pleasure in them. As the eternal destiny of souls is in the balance, fill us, Holy Spirit, and make us like Jesus.

The Blessing and Blight of Alternative Power

"...without Me you can do nothing."

John 15:5

When we experience a power failure in the physical realm, having alternative power can save the day, and even save lives. In the spiritual realm, we should never have a power failure. It happens, not because of the Generator, but because of the recipient.

Scripture reminds us that "His divine power has granted to us everything pertaining to life and godliness" (2 Peter 1:3, NASB). We are urged to live by "the exceeding greatness of His power toward us who believe, according to the working of His mighty power" (Ephesians 1:19). We have access to ultimate, supernatural, and uninterrupted power.

Plugging In to the Wrong Source

Yet, I find that we so easily rely on various forms of alternative power when we face the battles of daily life. This was illustrated to me recently as I read in 2 Chronicles 25:5-13. Amaziah, the king of Judah, had an adequate army of 300,000 as he prepared for war. Yet he still hired 100,000 soldiers to assist him in his military endeavors. A prophet of God told him that if he chose to rely on the additional troops, he would lose the battle, because "the Lord was not with them." Amaziah had already paid them an equivalent of 4 tons of silver. The account reads like this: "Amaziah asked the man of God, 'But what should I do about the silver I paid to hire the army of Israel?' The man of God replied, 'The LORD is able to give you much more than this!'" (2 Chronicles 25:9-10, NLT).

Amaziah sent the 100,000 soldiers away and went on to win the battle without his "alternative power plan." Sadly, he did not learn his lesson and immediately reverted to the use of his own power. He shamefully set up the gods of the defeated armies as his own gods, and rejected the correction of the prophet sent by the one true God to warn him.

Alternative human power is so available to us today. It is convenient, and it makes a lot of sense. It is enthusiastically recommended to us by other believers. It is promoted in our Christian magazines, leadership conferences, and pragmatic religious culture.

Trusting in Primary Power

To set aside alternative power choices may be costly, as it was to Amaziah, because we are often well down the road of pragmatism when we realize it is a tragic trajectory. It is at this point that we must obey the voice of the Spirit and exercise complete trust in the primary power source.

Offers of alternative power are nothing new. In the early church, Paul opposed those who offered alternative power through the human works of circumcision and keeping the law. Paul stood with firm resolve, pointing out the contrast and trusting in the real power of the Christian life. He wrote, "Look out for the dogs, look out for the evildoers, look out for those who mutilate the flesh. For we are the circumcision, who worship by the Spirit of God and glory in Christ Jesus and put no confidence in the flesh—though I myself have reason for confidence in the flesh also. If anyone else thinks he has reason for confidence in the flesh, I have more" (Philippians 3:2-4, ESV).

I don't know about you, but my heart longs to walk in the way of the true circumcision, as I put no confidence in the flesh. My flesh is so often drawn toward the logical, clever, intelligent, relevant, and natural. But these are too often contrary to a full-hearted trust in the sufficiency of Jesus Christ.

Alternative power is a blessing in the physical realm. In the Spiritual realm it is blight. May God give us wisdom to know the difference every day of our lives as we trust Him to live in and through us in the fullness of His unparalleled and unfailing power.

Looking for Good in All the Right Places

"No one is good but One, that is, God."

Mark 10:18

Without any doubt, life can be tough and seem futile at times. Whether we observe the apparent hopelessness of world politics or simply look at the circumstances of our inner circle, it is apparent that we have enough pain and disappointment to go around.

I often feel this weight when I am sitting with a sick parishioner, counseling the broken heart of a desperate parent, or praying with the deeply discouraged. Even as I write this, our own family is struggling through the process of losing a family member. Life brings its burdens swiftly.

The Bible says of the Lord, "You open Your hand, they are filled with good" (Psalm 104:28). Life may have hardships, but His goodness never changes. A proper perspective lies in our answer to two questions: "Where am I looking?" and "What am I thinking?"

I have often said, "Discouragement is a temporary loss of perspective." We are human and prone to look to the wrong source for some thing good. If we are not careful, we can start expecting good from the sources that never satisfy. People, circumstances, weather, health, bank accounts, careers, events, and earthly pleasure cannot provide ultimate happiness. All too often we emulate the guy who stands in front of a vending machine after depositing his three quarters, expecting a new car to pop out. (Can you clarify a little bit? I'm not sure I really understand this.)

A Right Perspective

The Psalmist declared, "I will lift up my eyes to the hills — From whence comes my help? My help comes from the LORD Who made heaven and earth" (Psalm 121:1-2). Psalm 145:15-16 again declares, "The eyes of all look expectantly to You, and You give them their food in due season. You open Your hand and satisfy the desire of every living thing."

It is important to look past the problems, perils, and pains of this life to see the good hand of God. The truth of God's character never changes with the wind. We look to Him as our ultimate and only source of real goodness. He wants to pour his goodness into our hearts everyday. The question is not one of His goodness, but of where we are looking for that goodness and whether we will recognize it or not.

This also means fixing our thoughts not on what we see, experience or feel, but on what we know to be true. We each must ask ourselves "What am I thinking?" Isaiah 26:3-4 (ESV) reminds us, "You keep him in perfect peace whose mind is stayed on you because he trusts in you. Trust in the LORD forever, for the LORD GOD is an everlasting rock."

Finding True Satisfaction

Life may feel bad, but God is good. Life seems unjust, but God is just. Life feels out of control, but God is sovereign. The one who fixes his mind on the things that are true recognizes and receives goodness. In a recent prayer gathering, I commented on how the Lord had satisfied the deep needs and longings of our hearts, as only He can do. I repeated the truth of God's word, "You open your hand and satisfy the desire of every living thing." I suggested to the people that we take some time to thank the Lord for the satisfaction He had accomplished in us by opening His hand of provision.

We each would finish the sentence, *'Lord, you have opened your hand and satisfied my desire for . . ."*

God's people cried out:

> *"Lord, You have opened Your hand and satisfied my desire for forgiveness."*
> *"Lord, You have opened Your hand and satisfied my desire for acceptance."*
> *"Lord, You have opened Your hand and satisfied my desire for joy."*
> *"Lord, You have opened Your hand and satisfied my desire for peace."*

These responses went on, and were as personal and unique as the depths of each heart. We were amazed at God's goodness as He opened His hands to us. He has opened them. He is opening them. He will open them. And you will be filled with good.

Swords and Bows

*"We have heard with our ears, O God, Our fathers have
told us, The deeds You did in their days, In days of old:
You drove out the nations with Your hand, But them
You planted; You afflicted the peoples, and cast them out
For they did not gain possession of the land by their own
sword, Nor did their own arm save them; But it was Your
right hand, Your arm, and the light of Your countenance,
Because You favored them."*

Psalm 44:1-3 (ESV)

I am struck by the clarity of how so many Biblical exploits were and
were not accomplished. Victorious battles for God's people were not
the result of human skill, human swords, or the magnitude of human
armies. They were acts of God's almighty hand. We see his determination to bless, and to extend his mighty right arm because of His love.
We read of this truth all throughout the Old Testament, and particularly in Psalm 44: 4 (ESV) "You are my King, O God; ordain salvation
for Jacob". The victory will clearly come from God. And His people
clearly acknowledge it.

The Psalm continues, inspiring us with more than just what God has
done, but with the possibilities of what God will do: "Through you we
push back our enemies; through your name we trample our foes. I
do not trust in my bow, and my sword does not bring me victory; but
you give us victory over our enemies, and you put our adversaries to
shame. In God we make our boast all day long, and we will praise your
name forever" (vv. 5-8, ESV).

God, by the authority of His name, pushes back our enemies, tramples our foes, and gives us ultimate victory, so that we will boast in Him all day long. But for this to occur, we cannot trust in our bows or swords. I often wonder: What is the sword in my hand that so easily becomes a false solution for my troubles? What is the bow at my disposal? What is it that tempts me to solve problems and overcome obstacles on my own?

May the Lord give us wisdom to discern the fine line between our routine self-reliance and a radical reliance on Christ. It seems to me that God wants to bless our lives in so many ways. However, when we are still trusting in swords and bows, we restrict His power and hinder His unique glory at work in and through us. Throw yourself onto the Savior today, and cling to Him always.

The Assurance of Love

"There is no fear in love; but perfect love casts out fear."

1 John 4:18

Recently I've been intrigued with chapter ten in the book of Daniel. Here we read of Daniel being overwhelmed by the vision he received from the Lord (10:1-3). Scripture presents a powerful picture of the pre-incarnate Christ appearing to Daniel in response to his fasting and prayers in order to strengthen his faith (10:4-9).

The chapter details conversations between the angel Gabriel and Daniel, through which Daniel gains understanding of an intense battle in the spiritual realm, and then receives strength and insight for his life (vv. 10-20). All of this may sound a bit ethereal, but think about how practical these ideas really are to our lives.

Our Needs in Battle

Every serious Christian committed to a biblical ministry and vision can get overwhelmed with the stress and magnitude of the task (See 2 Corinthians 1:8). Like Daniel, our greatest need in times of desperation is a fresh vision of the living Christ (Hebrews 12: 1-2; Revelation 1:12-18). We are all part of an unseen battle in the spiritual realm, and we all need God to give us strength and reassurance in the fight (2 Corinthians 12:9).

In the midst of this story we find a powerful theme. Three times in this part of Scripture, the Lord reassures Daniel of His love for him. Notice the descriptions: "At the beginning of your supplications the command went out, and I have come to tell you, for you are greatly beloved; therefore consider the matter, and understand the vision" (9:23). "O Daniel, man greatly beloved, understand the words that I speak to you, and stand upright, for I have now been sent to you" (10:11). "O man greatly beloved, fear not! Peace be to you; be strong, yes, be strong" (10:19).

Now think about this for a moment. If a great prophet like Daniel needed to receive this repeated message from the Lord, don't you think we need it too?

You Are Deeply Loved

I will never forget reading this passage a few years ago and being brought to tears with a fresh sense of God's love for me. I realized that by resting in that assurance, I was able to experience a deep abiding peace and stand with real strength in the midst of life's battles. Rejoice! Because of Christ, you are highly esteemed. You are deeply loved. When your vision is overwhelming, your strength is gone, and you are filled with fear, you are deeply loved. He cannot love you any more because He already loves you to the limits of love. You will never do anything to cause Him to love you any less, because His love is not based on you, nor does it hinge on you. It is rooted in His character, and it is His choice for you in Christ.

God's love is irrevocable and unconditional. Indeed, love is the very nature of God (1 John 4:8). It is on the basis of this truth that we are called to live a life marked by love (Ephesians 5:2), to love freely because He first loved us (1 John 4:19), and to keep ourselves in the love of God (Jude 21). God loves you deeply. Just as Daniel needed to hear this assurance of love over and again, we must also hear it continually.

Presenting Jesus in a Special Effects Culture

"For I determined not to know anything among you except Jesus Christ and Him crucified."

1 Corinthians 2:2

As I write this, the second installment of The Chronicles of Narnia films has been released in theatres. All of the advance promotions indicated that Prince Caspian was even better than The Lion, the Witch and the Wardrobe. From what I read and heard, the reason it was better had to do with the special effects, not the message or the acting.

I did see Prince Caspian. As expected, I enjoyed it very much. I suppose the special effects were superior to the previous film. Of course, I really enjoyed the message, which spoke of the folly of relying on our own wisdom and strength to fight the battles of life and the need to wait for Christ's power and His timing as we seek to live in victory.

Yet as I sat there, I kept thinking about that "special effects" issue. This was on my mind because I had been memorizing 1 Corinthians 2:1-5 with some men in my Wednesday morning leadership study. The passage reads,

> *"And I, brethren, when I came to you, did not come with excellence of speech or of wisdom declaring to you the testimony of God. For I determined not to know anything among you except*

Jesus Christ and Him crucified. I was with you in weakness, in fear, and in much trembling. And my speech and my preaching were not with persuasive words of human wisdom, but in demonstration of the Spirit and of power, that your faith should not be in the wisdom of men but in the power of God."

Honestly, even as I write this, I am not sure how to resolve the profound contrast between this powerful passage and the reality of our special effects world. I celebrate Walden Media's efforts to get wholesome, spiritually meaningful films like Prince Caspian into the mainstream of Hollywood. Others are doing the same effectively. But I wonder about the transition from the Saturday night movie to the Sunday morning service. How should the church respond?

Imitating the Special Effects?

It seems there is a tendency for the church to respond by "imitation." We try to create church services with special effects like smoke, lights, mirrors, video, more creative music, and anything else we can muster to impress the crowd.

I see two problems with this. First, it is usually a cheap imitation. The bottom line is that the church cannot compete with Hollywood at their game. We are out-spent, out-promoted, and we cannot match the technology and talent of the Hollywood industry on their field of special effects productions.

The second problem is obvious. The truth of 1 Corinthians 2:1-5 is clear. Paul communicates a resolute aversion to impressing people with superior communication techniques. He denounces persuasive cleverness and the use of the world's best wisdom in trying to communicate the truth of Christ. He rejects all kinds of emotional and intellectual manipulation. He instead chooses an attitude of weakness and inadequacy, locking in to a demonstration of the Spirit and His power. Paul's goal is that the faith of converts would "rest," or stand firm, on the foundation of the power of God, not the wisdom and cleverness of the world.

Our attempts to become increasingly high-tech, impressive, and clever have yielded paltry results at best. Even with all of our new abilities and unprecedented spending, the Christian influence has lost substantial ground. In the last decade, church attendance has fallen twelve percent across the board in the United States, and the number of those who classify themselves as irreligious has doubled. Investing billions of dollars in enhancing our impressiveness has proven to be a failed investment.

(Part Two)

Presenting Jesus in a Special Effects Culture

"Beware lest anyone cheat you through philosophy and empty deceit, according to the tradition of men, according to the basic principles of the world, and not according to Christ."

Colossians 2:8

If imitation is not the answer, then our best choice is to transcend the special effects approach. Only true Christianity, operating in the power of the Holy Spirit, can actually supersede the glamour and entertainment of computer-generated presentations. I believe Paul's teaching in 1 Corinthians 2:1-5 (and the verses that follow) gives us the sense of how this can really happen.

To "transcend" means to "rise above, go beyond or overpass; to exceed in excellence, elevation, extent or degree." In a theological sense, it carries the idea of being "above and independent of the universe, time, etc..." How can this happen? Let's reflect on Paul's determination and declaration in the passage.

A Singular Message

We can transcend a special effects culture though the power of a Singular Message - Paul resolves not to adapt impressive human wisdom and methodology in his ministry. He asserts, "For I determined not to

know anything among you except Jesus Christ and Him crucified."
Our firm conviction about the uniqueness, superiority, and sufficiency
of Jesus Christ is at the heart of the difference in our approach. If we
lose our belief in the power of the cross, we have lost the excellence of
what we offer, and we might as well all go to work for Disney or Pixar.

In Colossians 2:8-10, Paul warns us,

> *"Beware lest anyone cheat you through philosophy and empty
> deceit, according to the tradition of men, according to the basic
> principles of the world, and not according to Christ. For in Him
> dwells all the fullness of the Godhead bodily; and you are com-
> plete in Him, who is the head of all principality and power."*

Paul offers this warning because he is convinced of the surpassing
reality of who Jesus is and what He offers. Consider Paul's depiction:

> *"He is the image of the invisible God, the firstborn over all
> creation. For by Him all things were created that are in heaven
> and that are on earth, visible and invisible, whether thrones or
> dominions or principalities or powers. All things were created
> through Him and for Him. And He is before all things, and in
> Him all things consist" (Colossians 1:15-17).*

The film industry can offer powerful but temporary stimulation and
entertainment through special effects. Only the living Christ can offer
lasting transformation through the transcendence of His life and message. As a result, we can join Paul in this resolve: "But God forbid that
I should boast except in the cross of our Lord Jesus Christ, by whom
the world has been crucified to me, and I to the world" (Galatians
6:14).

We can transcend a special effects culture through the power of *simple
presentation* - Notice Paul's intentional desire to be unimpressive. He
uses descriptions like "weak," "fearful," and "trembling" to capture his
plan to be unimpressive in human terms.

It has been said, "When you make an impression, that is the impression you make." We will not attract the world to the power of the cross by trying to impress them with ourselves. I like to quote Jim Cymbala, who often says, "It is hard for me to be clever and make Jesus beautiful at the same time."

Weakness is a choice – and a good one for the church. A humble estimate of ourselves and our methods will help us bring more attention to the glory and transcendence of the cross. If we try to polish, decorate, promote, and embellish the "jars of clay," we could detract from the real impressiveness of the "treasure" within (2 Corinthians 4:5-7).

Supernatural Reliance

We can transcend a special effects culture through the power of a *supernatural reliance.* Last time I checked, the battery level of the "demonstration of the Spirit and of power" has not diminished in any sense. This was Paul's reliance. He goes on in 1 Corinthians 2 to describe the amazing and unlimited wisdom and enablement of the Spirit of God in our lives. He reminds us that "we haven't seen nothin' yet" compared to all the Spirit can really accomplish in and through us.

Admittedly, everything about our flesh wants to impress people with the packaging and presentations of our culturally relevant religion. But this proves to be our great mistake.

We don't play by those rules. We don't really even play on that field. Instead, we can live, minister, and communicate in a transcendent realm. The key to that realm is our own weakness, which leads us to being enamored with the cross – with full confidence in the message that is beyond special effects.

It has been said, "What it takes to reach people is what it takes to keep them." If our "bag of tricks" is the key to reaching them, then our tricks need to get better and our bag bigger. But if, like Paul, we can make it our resolve that the faith of those we reach will rely "on the power of God and not the wisdom of men," then all we have to do is to keep tapping into and walking in the sufficiency of that power.

What to do with all the Tools?

Yet, the fact is, we are living in the twenty–first century, not the first. We do have an enormous amount of tools at our disposal. As I speak to church leaders around the nation, I address the tension with this statement:

There is a difference between 'using' the tools and 'depending' on the tools. And the acid test of which one we are doing is the prayer level of our lives and our churches.

I truly believe that authentic, biblical prayer is our declaration of dependence on Christ rather than on our own best efforts. Real prayer announces our weakness – and glories in the power of the cross. Prayer keeps our reliance off our own versions of "special effects" and calls us to a transcending influence on people that cannot be explained in terms of visuals, audio, or dramatic sizzle.

So there is a fine line between a healthy "use" of the tools and an actual reliance on those tools. For me, 1 Corinthians 2:1-5 holds the key. That is why I am memorizing the passage. That is why I am asking a group of men to join me – and hold me accountable. That is why I am seeking to make the focus on Christ the heart of all I do in ministry.

Pray for me to that end – as I pray for you. Let's enjoy the entertainment value of the special effects and celebrate those who use them to communicate wholesome messages. But in our hearts, let's seek transcendence as we trust the Lord for the transformation Christ offers to our hurting and spiritually empty world.

The Three Good Questions in Eternity

"Be faithful until death, and I will give you the crown of life."

Revelation 2:10

Life is full of questions that stir our soul everyday. Some are deep, while others are quite shallow. Some questions are birthed out of our quest for meaning; others are a function of mere curiosity. Important as earthly questions might be, the core questions we must answer in eternity loom much greater.

Over the years, I have grappled with the most important questions for this side of eternity. My first book, *The Seven Most Important Questions You'll Ever Answer*, reflects the idea that our most important inquiries in this life are these:

- Who is God? (Theology)
- Who am I? (Identity)
- Why am I here? (Purpose)
- What really matters? (Values)
- Where am I going? (Vision)
- What shall I do? (Priorities)
- How shall I do it? (Goals)
- When shall I do it? (Time)

The goal of the book was to help find and apply biblical answers for these core issues of the soul.

But as I think about our inevitable destination in eternity, I am reminded of what I believe are the three essential questions God will ask (or at least, three issues that will be at the core of divine evaluation).

Question One:
What did you do with My Son?
(The Good Confession Issue - Salvation)

The entrance to heaven is singularly connected to one's response to the offer of salvation through Jesus Christ. In John 14:6 Jesus said, "I am the way, the truth, and the life. No one comes to the Father except through Me." Acts 4:12 states, "Nor is there salvation in any other, for there is no other name under heaven given among men by which we must be saved."

The Bible describes our positive response to the salvation call as a "good confession" (1 Timothy 6:12). As Romans 10:9-10 states, "If you confess with your mouth the Lord Jesus and believe in your heart that God has raised Him from the dead, you will be saved. For with the heart one believes unto righteousness, and with the mouth confession is made unto salvation." This is the first issue of eternity.

Question Two:
What did you do with what I gave you?
(The Good Works Issue - Stewardship)

For those who have responded positively with the good confession, the next question concerns their good works. Ephesians 2:10 tells us, "For we are His workmanship, created in Christ Jesus for good works, which God prepared beforehand that we should walk in them." Of course, as the previous verse states, He saves us for good works, whereby His Spirit gifts, empowers, and uses us for His glory.

We are all stewards of the manifold grace of God (1 Peter 4:10) and are responsible to diligently serve the Lord and others with all He has entrusted to us. We will give an account for what we have done and either lose or gain rewards in eternity.

Question Three:
Were you "good and faithful" in life?
(The Good Heart Issue - Sincerity)

In Matthew 25, the Bible presents the parable of the stewards. As we have just stated, they were responsible to do something productive and right with what had been entrusted to them. To the diligent, the Lord says, "Well done, good and faithful servant you have been faithful over a few things, I will make you ruler over many things. Enter into the joy of your lord."

The diligent stewardship of these servants occurred because they were "good" and "faithful." I believe this goes deeper than just actions – it reflects the heart of servants who will be graciously rewarded. A good character matters. The good treasure of the heart is the source of good words (Luke 6:45). That same gospel speaks of the soil of a good heart that receives God's word and bears fruit (Luke 8:15). The Bible speaks often of an honorable life, which is marked by a "good conscience" (1 Timothy 1:15, 19; 1 Peter 3:16). We are to hold fast to what is good (1 Thessalonians 5:21) and trust the Lord to establish us in "every good word and work" (2 Thessalonians 2:17). As a result we will be "rich in good works" (1 Timothy 6:18), "prepared for every good work" (2 Timothy 2:21), and "zealous for good works" (Titus 2:14). We read in 1 Peter 4:19 that we can "commit" (our) souls to Him in doing good, as to a faithful Creator."

The fruit of a faithful life also matters. In eternity, it will count that we have been faithful in our walk with the Lord, in our service, and in our love for the people God has put into our lives. Our fame or fortune will not matter, but our faithfulness to Christ will remain. In

Revelation 2:10, the Lord says to persecuted and suffering saints, "Be faithful until death, and I will give you the crown of life" (NASB).

So "let us run with endurance the race that is set before us, looking unto Jesus, the author and finisher of our faith, who for the joy that was set before Him endured the cross" (Hebrews 12:1- 2).

Just as a runner expects a prize at the end of a race, as a student expects a test at the end of the semester, or as a traveler expects a fee after several days in a parking garage – let us remember that at the conclusion of this life the evaluation will be clear. The issues of salvation, stewardship, and sincerity will matter. These are the questions we should anticipate and aim for as we live each and every day in Christ.

God's Reputation – Our Resolve

"But the end of all things is at hand; therefore be serious and watchful in your prayers."

1 Peter 4:7

These days God's holiness and the honor of His name are disgraced in abundance. Not only is Christ's name taken in vain with great frequency in daily conversations and throughout the media, but the attacks on His truth and trustworthiness are pervasive. These attacks are both overt and subtle.

Cultural Attacks on Faith

On one hand, books that aggressively belittle people of faith are populating the New York Times best-seller list in unprecedented fashion. Authors like Sam Harris, Christopher Hitchens, David Mills, Dorion Sagan, and Richard Dawkins are unashamed in their demeaning of faith and their exaltation of atheistic reason. People by the millions are reading these books.

Cynic and agnostic Bill Maher recently released a new documentary that attacks faith. One news writer described it as "a scathing, searing, stabbing, scabrous, sacrilegious attack on Divinity, Devotion, Prayer, and the Supreme Power."

More subtle, but in some ways more dangerous, is the fact that the fastest-growing church in America is the "church" of Oprah Winfrey. Her global classroom, featuring new-age author Eckhart Tolle, is encouraging millions to find their purpose in life apart from Jesus Christ. Oprah has been overt in her denial of the uniqueness of Jesus and the supreme honor of His name.

One right-wing author describes all of this as a pervasive "Christophobia" that marks a growing disdain of Christians, people of faith, and the God in whom they trust[8]. We live in a nation where the number of those who describe themselves as "irreligious" has doubled in the last ten years.

The Honor of His Word

Of course, all of this stirs my heart concerning our desperate need for revival in America. It also makes me jealous for the honor of Christ's name. That is natural. When we love someone, we are deeply disturbed by the disgracing of their name.

As I think of this, three key ideas come to mind. First, God is able to protect His own reputation. Isaiah 48:11 says, "For My own sake, for My own sake, I will do it; For how should My name be profaned? And I will not give My glory to another."

Recently I have noticed that when King Uzziah played fast and loose with God's holiness in 2 Chronicles 26:16–23 by taking on the priest's role in the temple, the Lord struck him with leprosy, and he died. When Herod was being praised as a god, and received that praise rather than rejecting this misguided worship, the Lord struck him down (Acts 12:20-24). There are many other examples like this. The point is that when He chooses, God can act in a clear and decisive manner to protect the honor of His name. This is His business, not ours.

Second, He is more concerned with how His own people dishonor His name than with how unbelievers mock Him. In a brief review of the biblical accounts that express God's concern for His name, they relate specifically to the need to judge His own people of Israel because they were defaming His honor. It seems He expects this kind of treatment from pagans and new age gurus. But when those who claim to know Him and represent His word dishonor Him – that seems to be when He acts to chastise and correct. The Old Testament accounts of the Israelites provide many examples. There are also examples of dishonor in the New Testament. In Acts 5, we see an unusual expression of this as God judged Ananias and Sapphira for dishonoring Him with their lies among the believers.

When the Apostle Peter spoke of the hostility of the world and the suffering of Christians as a result, he said something very profound. "For the time has come for judgment to begin at the house of God; and if it begins with us first, what will be the end of those who do not obey the gospel of God? Now, 'If the righteous one is scarcely saved, where will the ungodly and the sinner appear?' Therefore let those who suffer according to the will of God commit their souls to Him in doing good, as to a faithful Creator" (1 Peter 4:17-19). My application is simply that, as bad as it may get out there, the Lord still wants to clean His own house first. In time He will take care of all opponents of the Gospel – and He will do it thoroughly.

In the meantime, Peter says we are to commit our souls in doing good, as to a faithful Creator. This is a great segue to my third observation. When a culture becomes hostile, God's holiness is being defamed, and His hand of judgment is on display, believers must return to "position one" – on their face in His presence.

Isaiah 6 tells us that in "The year that King Uzziah died" Isaiah saw the Lord in His temple. As we have read, the prophet experienced a fresh understanding of God's holiness and power, repented of his own sin, and yielded fully to the call of God to continue with the mission. Similarly, after Herod was struck down for receiving the worship that is reserved for God alone, the leaders in Antioch were found "ministering to the Lord" as they fasted and worshipped (Acts 13:1-2). They also surrendered to the call of the Spirit to keep going out with the message; this was when the Spirit commissioned Saul and Barnabas for their mission.

Representing His Honor

In summary, when we have a concern with God's reputation in this world, we can rest in knowing that He is able to fend for Himself. We must continually look at our own lifestyle and behavior, knowing that we represent Him in this world and that our lives and testimonies are His primary concern. Then we must resolve to continually seek Him, experience His presence, surrender to His call, and stay on task.

Again, Peter summarized it well when he addressed Christians in a hostile culture. In 1 Peter 4:7 he wrote, "But the end of all things is at hand; therefore be serious and watchful in your prayers." He went on to tell them to love one another, to be hospitable, to refrain from grumbling, and to stay on task in serving in God's power and grace. Then he said, "That in all things God may be glorified through Jesus Christ, to whom belong the glory and the dominion forever and ever. Amen."

Regardless of what is going on around us, we have the calling and privilege of making sure that what is going on among us and within us honors His name and brings glory to Him in this world. So let Maher, Harris, Dawkins, Tolle and the rest do their thing. Our lives and godly behavior are really the greater force for God's good and glory in this world.

A Sensible Forgiveness
"But if you do not forgive, neither will your Father in heaven forgive your trespasses."

Mark 11:26

I am convinced that a primary strategy of the enemy is to destroy Christian relationships and specifically encourage a spirit of unforgiveness. Twice the New Testament speaks of this as the primary area where our spiritual enemy gains advantage over Christians. In speaking of the dangers of unresolved anger and coddled bitterness, Paul warns us not to give a foothold to the devil in our lives (Ephesians 4:16-31). In speaking of the need for forgiveness, Paul also warns that we cannot let the devil take advantage of us (2 Corinthians 2:11).

The Importance of Forgiveness
We know how important forgiveness is because we realize how many people truly need to experience forgiveness in this life. Ernest Hemmingway writes about a Spanish father who decided to reconcile with his son who had run away to Madrid[9]. In an attempt to locate his son, the father took out an ad in the El Liberal newspaper: "PACO, MEET ME AT HOTEL MONTANA NOON TUESDAY. ALL IS FORGIVEN, PAPA." Paco is a common name in Spain, and when the father went to the square he found 800 young men named Paco waiting for their fathers.

We know that forgiveness is commanded, even "seventy times seven" times (Matthew 18:21-22). Forgiveness is essential to our commitment to be like Christ. We are required to extend forgiveness if we are to enjoy the full experience of forgiveness with our Heavenly Father (Mark 11:26).

The Sensibility of Forgiveness

Of course, because God is wise and His ways are always good, forgiveness also makes sense. It leads to a sensible freedom, a sensible fellowship, and a sensible future.

A Sensible Freedom – When we forgive, we enjoy a practical freedom. It's been said that, "Forgiveness doesn't make the other person right, it makes you free." Unforgiveness is a "control mechanism" whereby we try to exercise some kind of emotional jurisdiction and power over the situation and the other person. When we forgive we become free of all the exhausting attempts to manage the situation in our flesh. We are free to trust God for the outcome.

As author Phil Ryken[10] has written, "Forgiveness brings great joy, not only to the forgiven, but especially to the forgiver. The Greek term for 'forgiveness' (aphiemi) comes from a word that means 'to let go.'" Forgiveness is a release, a letting go of self-destructive feelings such as anger, bitterness, and revenge.

All of us experience pain in life. We can be deeply hurt by abandonment, criticism, lies, slander, abusive words, and disappointed expectations. Pain is inevitable. Bitter misery is optional. When we know that God gives us the grace to forgive and be forgiven, but refuse to make that choice, we live in unnecessary, self-inflicted pain. That makes no sense.

A Sensible Fellowship – God created us with a deep need for intimacy with Himself and others. Forgiveness opens up the supply line of indescribable blessing both in our relationships with God and with other people.

Often, the very person toward whom we are angry or bitter is one from whom we need to receive love, affirmation, and grace. Unforgiveness keeps us from enjoying the benefits of this relationship. It is like a person who intentionally starves himself to death while a table full of delicious and nutritious food is within reach.

A failure to forgive soon turns into bitterness, which in time also defiles and wounds many other people (Hebrews 12:15). No rational, loving person would detonate a hand grenade at a gathering of friends and family. Yet an unforgiving spirit has that very effect spiritually, emotionally, and relationally on anyone close to an embittered person.

I've heard it said that unforgiveness is like drinking poison and expecting the other person to die. Not only does anger and bitterness eventually kill us emotionally, it negatively impacts our very ability to relate to others in a healthy way. In a world where we all need the support, grace, counsel, and love of other believers, forgiveness makes a lot of sense.

A Sensible Future – God's forgiveness has unleashed a real and abiding hope in our lives. Forgiveness always brings hope to troubled relationships. Conversely, unforgiveness kills hope. An embittered heart sees only the worst in others, in themselves, in situations, and in the future. This pessimism is in opposition to the truth about God and His plan for our lives.

A life that chooses forgiveness, extends blessing, and pursues peace is a life that will be richly rewarded by Christ. The person living this kind of life has been a careful and thoughtful steward of God's grace. It just makes sense to live this way.

Forgiven Much to Forgive Much

In Luke 7:47, Jesus explained that when we are forgiven much, we love much. The great English preacher Martin Lloyd-Jones said, "Whenever I see myself before God and realize something of what my blessed Lord has done for me at Calvary, I am ready to forgive anybody anything. I cannot withhold it. I do not even want to withhold it."[11]

Ken Sande, in his book *The Peacemaker*, writes, "We take God's forgiveness for granted when we stubbornly withhold our forgiveness from others. In effect, we behave as though others' sins against us are more serious than our sins against God."[12]

When the power of the Gospel has made sense to us – forgiveness makes sense. It is the good and right thing to do.

Henry Ward Beecher stated that, "Every man should keep a fair-sized cemetery in which to bury the faults of his friends."[13] It is God's will that our cemetery of forgetfulness grows as our commitment to truly and completely forgive increases. The devil hates it when we truly understand these things. But, it just makes sense.

Christians Gone Crazy

"You are the salt of the earth; but if the salt loses its flavor, how shall it be seasoned? It is then good for nothing but to be thrown out and trampled underfoot by men."

Matthew 5:13

Every day, it seems, we read or hear another account of "Christian" people being caught doing things that are anything but Christian. People of "faith" are found guilty of fraud, fondling children, and faking the truth in a variety of ways. With tears, they admit to their scandals, sex-capades, and stealing, but give praise to God for the presence of Jesus in their lives. In the meantime, Christ weeps, His work suffers, the world laughs, and fellows Christians wonder what in the world is going on.

Examples Galore

In the process of writing my book Defying Gravity (How to Survive the Storms of Pastoral Leadership) I interviewed dozens of Christian leaders (not all pastors) about some of the challenges they have faced. I will never forget the response I received from Karen Covell, a television producer and author. She serves as the Director of the Hollywood Prayer Network, seeking to mobilize prayer for "the most influential mission field in the world" as she connects with intercessors around the world. Karen and her husband, Jim (also a producer and my best friend from junior high school) have led a weekly prayer meeting in their home for their colleagues for almost 25 years.

Not long ago, Karen discovered that a trusted friend and co-laborer for over 20 years, who handled HPN's finances, was "borrowing money" from HPN. By the time Karen discovered this it was almost too late to salvage the ministry. Suddenly she was in the situation of needing to decide how to handle her colleague, what to do to save the ministry, or whether she should just shut it all down and start over. She found herself struggling with the thought of rebuilding – knowing the commitment, time, effort, and fundraising that it would take. As I wrote about her brokenhearted journey of trying to salvage the ministry, I wondered, "How could someone do that to such a wonderful person and ministry?"

Of course, this is one of hundreds (maybe thousands) of stories that emerge every week across America involving "the faithful" and their woeful wrongdoings. I am not talking about a temper flare-up, speeding ticket, or failing to tithe. I am talking about major, public scandals that damage the faith of others because of the level of blatant duplicity involved. Whether it is a high-profile evangelist, a "Christian" politician, or a friend in our small group Bible study – it is all so very baffling. Let us try to make sense of it.

Humble Disclaimer

First, let's admit the need for humility and grace as we consider this issue. Every one of us has entertained a thought or contemplated an action that could have resulted in great harm to our testimony and pain to those we love. As Galatians 6:1 says, we need to consider ourselves "lest we also be tempted." God's grace instructs us all that "denying ungodliness and worldly lusts, we should live soberly, righteously, and godly in the present age" (Titus 2:12). Truly we can all say that, apart from His grace, "There go I."

Why Do "Christian" People Do Such Crazy Things?

While hardly a theological treatise or counseling session, I want to share a few thoughts about how other believers can misfire so badly.

False Profession – Sometimes people behave in blatantly non-Christian ways because they are non-Christians. Just as godly repentance does not register in their present behavior, neither did it register when they "made a decision" to become a Christian. Read Matthew chapter seven. Enough said.

Unsanctified Brokenness – Many people come to Christ but never really bring the brokenness of their past or present life under the power of the cross. For example, the baggage of uncrucified bitterness can lead to damaging decisions. The pain grows deep and eventually results in irrational, reactionary behavior that takes this unthinking believer from the frying pan of pain into the fire of widespread disgrace.

Another example might be the deep-seated dysfunction of an unsettled identity. Some Christians were raised with strong messages that their value was in how they appeared to others, what they possessed, or what things they achieved. Rather than living out an identity that is solid and settled at the cross, they are still trying to prove an identity that some powerful figure told them they must prove. To find themselves, they risk losing their integrity and intimacy with Christ and others.

Skewed View of Holiness – Our present culture tempts us in many ways to redefine God's holiness. When we impose the acceptable behaviors of the day over the biblical picture of God's absolute holiness, we set ourselves up to justify unholy behavior. I have heard it said, "In the beginning God created man in His image. Ever since, we've been trying to return the favor."

Compartmentalized Behavior – Integrity is about a life where all the pieces fit together in authentic harmony and honesty. When compromise begins in some area of life, a person can begin to compartmentalize and believe that his behavior or thought patterns in one area are not necessarily related to other areas of life. Financial compromise gets isolated from family. Sexual misbehavior is tolerated as long as the individual serves at church. It is an approach that spells eventual disaster.

Seared Conscience – Some arrive at such a point of coddling a lying lifestyle that they actually yield their thoughts to the power of evil and no longer respond to the God-given voice of conscience. They develop a lifestyle of getting away with sin, with little remorse and minimal concern for the consequences.

A Godly Response

In the meantime, we must make the decision every day to find our strength for holy living and authentic witness in Christ alone. As He taught us, "Abide in Me, and I in you. As the branch cannot bear fruit of itself, unless it abides in the vine, neither can you, unless you abide in Me" (John 15:4).

Ephesians 5:8-10 reminds us, "For you were once darkness, but now you are light in the Lord. Walk as children of light (for the fruit of the Spirit is in all goodness, righteousness, and truth), finding out what is acceptable to the Lord." May we each resolve to walk the talk and manifest His light. Let us pray that the fruit of goodness, righteousness, and truth will be evident in our lives as we actively discover all that is acceptable to the Lord and avoid the pitfalls of this all-too-common crazy behavior.

(Part Two)

Christians Gone Crazy

"You are the salt of the earth; but if the salt loses its flavor, how shall it be seasoned? It is then good for nothing but to be thrown out and trampled underfoot by men."

Matthew 5:13

In part one of "Christians Gone Crazy" we considered the apparent frequency with which Christian people are caught doing crazy things that are anything but Christian. Perhaps the rapid release of juicy stories via cable television, the Internet, and Twitter just give greater visibility to this behavior. In any case, we evaluated the reasons for this behavior, seeking to do so with grace and honesty.

We want to consider the impact of these major missteps by fellow Christians as well as our response to these sad situations of moral malfunction.

What is the Impact of This Crazy Behavior?

It is good to prepare our minds with a survey of the consequences of ill-advised behaviors. Just as Proverbs describes the tragic outcome of bad moral choices, so should we regularly consider the negative impact of our displays of disobedience. This certainly encourages us to avoid the path of scandalous sin but also encourages praying for those who taste the bitter fruit of their spiritual failures.

Shame to Christ – The great tragedy of theses crazy escapades is the discredit they bring to the Savior's holy name. Christ's reputation is tarnished and disgrace has marred the work He died to establish. Some will use the bad behavior of believers to discount the claims of Christ. As Nietzsche stated, "I would believe in your redeemer if you lived as if you were redeemed."

Delight for Satan – The enemy always rejoices when he can trip up or throw down a Christ-follower, knowing he has ultimately broken the heart of Jesus. No one sets out to make Satan smile, but this is the true effect.

Shattered Relationships – Sin is described as the violation of a relationship – first with God, then with countless others who expressed confidence in the straying individual. To wander into the weeds of wanton behavior always involves the choice to hurt and violate the trust of people who love us.

Painful Earthly Consequences – Of course, depending on the area of sin, there are various consequences. Adultery can destroy a marriage and family. White-collar crime lands a man in jail. Drunk driving can result in fatal accidents. Genuine sorrow may evoke forgiveness from the family of the victim but it will not bring a life back.

Lost Eternal Reward – Ultimately, any earthly consequences are but a vapor compared to the loss of eternal joy and reward in the everlasting presence of the Lamb. Rewards in eternity are granted to the faithful who serve with pure motives and persevering faithfulness.

What Should We Do About This Craziness?

Humble our Hearts – If you have stumbled in some fashion that has brought open shame to the Lord, your family, His work, and your own reputation – genuine humility is the first step to recovery. Humility is the precursor to real repentance and change.

James 4:7-10 provides clear guidance for the wandered trying to find his way back home via that path of humility in the presence of the

Almighty:

> "Therefore submit to God. Resist the devil and he will flee from you. Draw near to God and He will draw near to you. Cleanse your hands, you sinners; and purify your hearts, you double-minded. Lament and mourn and weep! Let your laughter be turned to mourning and your joy to gloom. Humble yourselves in the sight of the Lord, and He will lift you up."

Humility is also in order toward our fellow man with whom we have been entangled or toward whom we have created the offences. The straying soul would do well to adopt the attitude promoted in Proverbs: "Go and humble yourself; plead with your friend. Give no sleep to your eyes, nor slumber to your eyelids. Deliver yourself like a gazelle from the hand of the hunter, and like a bird from the hand of the fowler" (Proverbs 6:3-5).

Learn our Lessons – The immediate season after a spiritual failure is one of the great moments for learning the lessons that result in genuine life change. Ask God to help you apply the salve of divine wisdom to the self-inflicted wounds of sin. Embrace the sorrow that leads to real, lasting repentance, not just the regret of being caught. Failure is a powerful teacher if we are willing to learn, recalibrate our senses, and resolve to avoid any return to the mire.

Watch our Steps – If you have been preserved by God's grace and your own common sense from scandalous sin, by all means, guard your thoughts, decisions, and deeds by resolute determination to honor Christ and His Word – every day.

Surround our Actions – Spiritual survivors do not go it alone. They have learned the value of accountability in every area of life. They embrace the wisdom of avoiding any appearance of evil and surrounding themselves with checks and balances in the areas of money, morality, and ministry activity.

Trust, but Verify – Realize that saints who just might do something stupidly scandalous surround you – and you could become part of the fallout. Yes, trust your fellow believers – but verify their behaviors through accountability, direct questions, and systems that will not tempt them to blow it in a weak moment. It is better to be criticized for careful scrutiny than to be stuck untangling the spaghetti of shameful stumbles and permanently damaged relationships.

Thank God for the Faithful

In spite of the reality of this craziness – the fact remains that every day millions of Christians remain faithful to Christ and His claims on their lives. For every crash-and-burn story there are multiplied thousands of godly saints whose stories of love, grace, and positive spiritual impact will never make the news.

We want to be among these faithful saints. The secret is that we abide in Christ, drawing our life from His sufficiency in and through us. He will bear the fruit of godly living through us, in spite of the trends and temptations of the day (John 15:5-10). Praise God that we do not have to succumb to crazy decisions and shameful behavior. We can live a life of abiding love for Him and selfless love toward others, which is always a choice for purity and perseverance. We can stand in the promise that He "always leads us in triumph in Christ, and through us diffuses the fragrance of His knowledge in every place" (2 Corinthians 2:14).

In closing, I think of how Paul wrote to Timothy about the crazy and perilous days that would come as time unfolds. The culture would be marked by people described as "lovers of themselves, lovers of money, boasters, proud, blasphemers, disobedient to parents, unthankful, unholy, unloving, unforgiving, slanderers, without self-control, brutal, despisers of good, traitors, headstrong, haughty, lovers of pleasure rather than lovers of God, having a form of godliness but denying its power" (2 Timothy 3:1-5). In spite of all this senselessness, Paul reminded Timothy of the sufficiency of the Word of God in his life and offered him the final exhortation he would ever pen to his young understudy: "But you should keep a clear mind in every situation. Don't be afraid of suffering for the Lord. Work at bringing others to Christ. Complete the ministry God has given you" (2 Timothy 4:5).

He knew Timothy could live a sane and sanctified life by the power of Christ, regardless of the times. So can you.

How's Your Outlook Working?

"Has God not chosen the poor of this world to be rich in faith and heirs of the kingdom which He promised to those who love Him?"

James 2:5

Imagine the current global population of almost seven billion people arranged in one massive single-file line. Picture yourself in the line. Regardless of how you rank in the American economic scale, you will be near the front of the line simply because you live in the United States.

Up the line are the people who have more than you. At the front you find people like Bill Gates, Warren Buffet, and other mega-billionaires. At the back of the line might be a 2-year-old-orphan girl from Sudan with a distended belly, taking her last breath due to extreme starvation. There are millions like her at the back of the line.

Here is the question: What is your outlook from your position in the line? Are you spending most of your energy looking up the line at those who have more than you? Are you investing energy looking down that line at those less fortunate? Is your approach working for you? How does it affect the way you live every day?

All of us have some very important options in our outlook from where we stand in the line.

Looking Up the Line?

It is customary for high-achieving Americans to spend most of our energy looking up the line. We are ambitious people. We are also bombarded by advertising and television shows that seek to convince us that the key to real happiness and significance is somewhere up the line.

If we spend most of our time looking up the line, comparing our situation with those who are more "rich and famous", we typically reap the internal fruit of ingratitude, discontent, greed, and even idolatry.

Looking Down the Line?

Most of the world is down the line...VERY far down the line. Unless you have traveled to some of the poverty-stricken nations, observed the masses of broken lives, and been touched by the sights and smells of human devastation, it can be hard to even imagine life for those billions who live "down the line" from you. It is not so hard to imagine friends and family who are not so far down the line, but who need help and encouragement from us.

If we do our best to focus down the line, cultivating a greater awareness of the deep spiritual, social, and materials needs of others, we usually become more grateful, humble, compassionate, and sacrificial in how we think and live.

Looking Below the Line?

It is also important to look below the line in both directions. Deeper than the surface appearances of wealth or poverty we often discover the real "happiness" factor of daily life. This "below the line" happiness has much to do with an authentic walk with Christ, quality relationships, gratitude for the simple gifts of life, and a willingness to choose joy in all circumstances. Both experience and the Bible tell us that moving up the line does not guarantee greater satisfaction. In fact, we usually find just the opposite can be true.

Jesus stated that a man's life does not consist of the things he possesses (Luke 12:15). Paul warns that a love for money is a root of all kinds of evil that can pierce our soul (1 Timothy 6:9-10). The Bible consistently honors the poor, not as an endorsement of poverty or laziness, but as recognition of the humble and gracious heart that is often exhibited by the less fortunate, even in tough circumstances.

Obviously, God blesses some people to move up the line so that they can use those blessings as stewards to advance His kingdom. Others are "driven" up the line by an ambition that eventually backfires and robs them of true well-being.

Looking Above the Line?

Probably the most important look is the upward look. Above the line of humanity is a good, sovereign, and just God. He knows where we are on the line. His providence allows us to be there. He knows the beginning from the end and our times are in His hands (Psalm 31:15). He will guide us as we move up or down the line.

Keeping our eyes focused on Him in humble trust and active faith is one of the keys to a healthy outlook. In obedience to His Word we should work hard, be aware of open doors, be generous stewards, diligently serve others, and let Him guide our steps as we live on the line.

Is Your Outlook Working?

As you live on the line of humanity, recognize the choices you have in your outlook. Choose the approach that works and cultivates a good and godly growth in your life. As I often say, "The hardest thing about the Christian life is that it is so daily." Every day we must ask God for the grace to choose the best perspective, and then trust Him as we seek to live faithfully and fruitfully on the line – and for the sake of eternity.

Is the Frog Cooked Yet?
"When the Son of Man comes, will He really find faith on the earth?"

Luke 18:8

Many times over the years I've read and heard church experts describe the American Church as a "frog in a kettle." The illustration tells us that if you drop a frog in a kettle of boiling water it will jump out immediately in reaction to the pain. On the other hand, if you put the frog in water that is room temperature, slowly heating it, the frog will remain in the kettle and eventually cook to death. Frankly, I do not know if this is actually true, but this is a good time to revisit the idea in light of the recent headlines about the decline of Christianity in our nation.

What the News Tells us About the Frog

Recently, Newsweek Magazine's cover story highlights current research about the decline of Christianity in America. In the article titled, "The End of Christian America", Jon Meacham commented extensively on the implications of the recent results of the American Religious Identification Survey[14]. Two core facts that have arrested everyone's attention are the findings that the percentage of self-identified Christians has fallen 10 percentage points since 1990 and the number of people willing to describe themselves as atheist or agnostic has increased about fourfold from 1990 to 2009.

Also in the news we found a riveting article in the Christian Science Monitor by Michael Spencer titled "The Coming Evangelical Collapse." This thoughtful article predicts that within 10 years there will be an accelerated collapse of Evangelical influence coupled with an open hostility toward Christians by our securely and religiously antagonistic culture[15].

In a recent speech in Turkey, our president boldly described the United States as a secular nation and not a Christian nation[16]. Clearly this signals a firm definition of our nation as a people no longer identified by strong Christian roots or values.

While people of faith are certainly not disappearing from the landscape of America, the trends certainly tell us that the water is getting hotter around the frog.

An Understanding of the Water

It is important that we understand that the water in which the frog is cooking is not the culture. The danger to the frog is not secularism, liberalism, or atheism. To believe this is to conclude that these worldviews are more powerful than the message of the cross.

I believe the water in which we are boiling is our own spiritual apathy, missional indifference, and prayerless irrelevance. In essence, the frog stands in danger of boiling in its own water. Just as Jesus warned some of the churches in Revelation chapters 2 & 3 about their precarious spiritual condition, we too must recognize our own need to take responsibility for the situation.

What the Frog Must Do

Personally, I am convinced that I must do all I can to encourage the church in vital renewal in these days. Further, I believe the American Church must seriously "hear what the Spirit is saying to the churches" (Revelation 2:7, 11, 17, 29; 3:6, 13, 22). Just as Christ's words to the seven churches of Revelation brought a stern wake-up call and, in some cases, words of comfort – so we need to try to understand His heart for our present condition in our nation.

Recognition – As we reflect on the objective findings of these recent studies we should carefully consider our response. What is more, we should see the data as merely symptomatic of even deeper concerns about our spiritual substance in the American church. Many of us have observed over many years the growing conformity to the world's practices and a business-oriented approach to ministry. We've had concerns that we are depending more on methods, technology, and human skill than on the power of the Spirit and the Word of God. We've observed our prayer-deprived congregations, knowing that at some point it would catch up to us. The water of our apathy has slowly come to a boil and it is imperative that we recognize it and act in obedience to the Spirit.

Repentance – I often say that the problem in our nation is not the pervasiveness of the darkness but the failure of the light. If darkness is advancing it is because the light is failing. Speaking to the churches in Revelation, Jesus repeatedly gave the command, "Repent or else" (Revelation 2:5, 16, 21, 21; 3:3, 19). My prayer is that the current state of affairs will motivate us all to turn from our self-reliance and self-satisfaction. My prayer is that God will allow us to turn from everything that might encourage our faith to rest on the wisdom of man rather than the power of God (1 Corinthians 2:5).

Resurgence – Jesus called the church at Ephesus that had left their first love to return to their first works (Revelation 2:5). He urged the church at Sardis to wake up from their dead state and to strengthen what remained (Revelation 3:3). He appealed to the lukewarm church at Laodicea to open the door of their lives to the presence of Christ and exchange their self-sufficiency for His best gifts (Revelation 3:17-20). At all costs, we too must sense His call to spiritual resurgence and genuine renewal during these crucial days. Of course, this is the mission and vision of Strategic Renewal.

Revival – Jesus challenged the churches in the book of Revelation to overcome, and offered them abundant promises if they did. I am mindful of John the Apostle's words in 1 John 5:4-5: "For whatever is born of God overcomes the world. And this is the victory that has overcome the world — our faith. Who is he who overcomes the world, but he who believes that Jesus is the Son of God?"

The Hope of Overcoming, Prayerful Faith

I am hopeful that these present times will motivate the truly regenerate Christ followers to overcome in faith. I am also persuaded that many who have attached themselves to the church in America in a spirit of convenience or entertainment will fall by the wayside.

Finally, I am reminded of Christ's story of the persistent widow in Luke 18:1-8 who serves as an example of His command that we should always pray, and not lose heart (v. 1). At the end of that passage He asks a penetrating and truly relevant question: "Nevertheless, when the Son of Man comes, will He really find faith on the earth?" In context, this faith is marked by a persevering prayerfulness.

These are the times that challenge us to consider the seriousness of that question and, by grace, to respond with a resounding "yes." May the Lord find us always praying, persevering, and trusting that the overcoming power of faith in His Gospel and His presence within us will make the difference in these defining moments for our lives, families, and nation.

Just One

*"I say to you that likewise there will be more joy
in heaven over one sinner who repents than over
ninety-nine just persons who need no repentance."*

Luke 15:7

Not long ago I had the honor of leading in a renewal conference hosted
by Central Wesleyan Church in Holland, MI. Paul Hontz, the senior
pastor, has served that fellowship for 30 years and led the church to
become one of the largest congregations of their denomination in the
U.S. How delightful to see a large and influential congregation so
hungry for a fresh movement of spiritual power and impact!

As Pastor Hontz sat with a friend and I in his office Sunday morning
before the services, I could not help but notice a small quote on the
wall. It read, "To the world you may just be one person, but to one
person you may be the world." Wow. I could not get that off my mind.

Real Impact

So many times we get confused about the nature of real impact in this
world. It seems that our culture is in a mad scramble for the top of the
pile. Notoriety. Fame. Recognition. These are the common pursuits of
driven people, both religious and secular. Yet we know all of this can
evaporate overnight and ultimately fade quickly from the radar screen
of real significance.

On the other hand, who can estimate the impact of a life that meaningfully touches just one soul for eternity? How can we quantify the example of a godly father to his son, or a caring mother to her daughter? How can we measure the influence of a Christ-like neighbor or work associate who really loves and cares for the folks around him? Can we really comprehend the loving investment of a Sunday School teacher in the life of a lonely, fatherless child?

The examples could go on endlessly. The point is that we cannot undermine the value of tuning in to the needs of just one person by becoming caught up in the grandiosity of the bigger and better pursuits in life.

Our Ultimate Example

Think of Jesus, individually selecting twelve awfully common men to become recipients of His discipleship investment. Remember His invitation to a single, stubby tax collector in a tree. Don't forget the obscure woman with the issue of blood, lost in a crowd of needy people, but singled out to receive heavenly healing power. Consider His advocacy for a sinful, guilty adulteress about to be stoned by the religious hypocrites. Feel the wonder of His determination – over and over again – to stop whatever He was doing to touch a broken body, to heed the call of a hurting parent whose child was suffering, and to engage in life-changing conversations with individuals beyond number.

To the world, He was just one person – but to one person, He became the world. I am among the millions touched by His individual love – and so are you. How appropriate that He would care so much that we should pass that love on to others – one soul at a time.

Our Necessary Focus

Even now, I remember the impact of the lyrics. The verses tell of grandious visions for ministry to the masses. The first verse spoke of standing on a vista and imagining all the people of the world, longing to tell each of them about Jesus. The second verse expresses a desire to visit all the sick and aged with a desire to minister to them with the truth new life in Christ. It also describes visiting the prisons of the world with a message of freedom in Christ. The final verse envisions traveling across the oceans and throughout the nations to tell of the light of Christ among those living in darkness.

Then, the chorus so beautifully and carefully says:

> *Oh, but Lord, remind me daily of my neighbor*
> *And those who may know me by my name*
> *If I forget the ones and think of millions*
> *It would be much more for me than eternal shame*[17]

Just one. That's all He asks us to focus on. Who will it be today? To the world you may just be one person – but to that person you may be the world. In that instance, show them Jesus. Their world will never be the same.

Losing Some to Gain More

"But what things were gain to me, these I have counted loss for Christ."

Philippians 3:7

One of my best sermons as a young college student came from Philippians 3:7-8, where Paul wrote:

> *"But what things were gain to me, these I have counted loss for Christ. Yet indeed I also count all things loss for the excellence of the knowledge of Christ Jesus my Lord, for whom I have suffered the loss of all things, and count them as rubbish, that I may gain Christ."*

I spoke passionately about how we needed to count our plans, people, and possessions as "rubbish" compared to knowing Christ. I even had the audience write down the specific descriptions of things they valued, and then challenged them to bring that piece of paper forward to deposit the list in a trashcan in front of the auditorium. I felt so inspired, and the sermon seemed to be truly effective.

Actually, my experience with the biblical text was very shallow. For any of us to say we have "suffered the loss of all things" is disingenuous in our prosperous American society where everything is about upward mobility and accumulation of more stuff. I was young at the time, with the promise of the world in front of me – so I knew very little about "loss." How could I really understand the depth of this passage? I was sincere, but shallow in my efforts to embrace and teach this passage.

Our good and loving God has a way of making truth real in our lives in order to make us more mature and authentic in our faith. He has kindly helped me in this way, allowing me to understand a little more about "losses" and "gains" in my spiritual pilgrimage.

Possessions, People, and Plans

Recently our family has experienced some fresh losses as a direct result of our obedience to the call of God on our lives. Because of our commitment to pursue full-time ministry with Strategic Renewal, we left the security of the senior pastor role and followed the Lord's direction to move to Virginia. In the process, I had to give up my plans for the security and "success" of a mega-church pastor.

Recently, we sold our home in Minnesota (after two long years of double mortgage payments). This was an answer to prayer. Along the way, we lost a lot of savings and all of our home equity. The reality of losing possessions for the sake of Christ is much more real today than it was in college.

In the last six months, we have lost the physical presence of all three of our children in our home as each one has followed the call of God to marriage, work, or school. This is a "gain" for each of them, and a blessing to Christ's kingdom, but the void parents feel is very real in seasons like this. We are learning to count even our children as "loss" for the sake of Christ and His purposes.

In a variety of other ways, our obedience to the call of God has involved loss of status, security, certainty, friendships, and even sleep. Of course, these losses are miniscule when contrasted with eternity's reward for obedient service. Compared to the painful "losses" others we know are experiencing right now, our sacrifice may seem trivial. I have friends who have lost a spouse, a career, all financial security, and even their health in recent days. Still, they love and serve Christ.

Trading Loss for Gain

Having said all of this, I am not whining – but I am seeking a deeper level of worship. Sure, times of self-pity and carnal regret can surface. At those moments I am reminded that a man's life does not consist of the abundance of his possessions (Luke 12:15) and that we must be willing to leave all, take up our cross, and follow Christ if we are to be classified as a true disciple (Luke 14:26-27).

Clearly, the trade-in is worth it – even though it is not easy. It is good to remember that with every loss, we can gain:

• A deeper knowledge of Christ, who was unencumbered by the trappings of this world. This knowledge is truly priceless (Philippians 3:7-8, 10).

• A mature and biblical perspective about the things that really matter in this life (Philippians 3:8).

• A powerful sense of Christ-reliance rather than self-reliance, where we discover the sufficiency of His work on the cross and His righteous life in us (Philippians 3:9).

• A new experience of the power of His resurrection, which brings new life out of death – and ultimate gain from our losses (Philippians 3:10).

• A fresh infusion of grace, that works most powerfully when we are weak (2 Corinthians 12:9-10).

Our losses in life are God's way of prying our fingers off our comfortable idols in order to free our hands to more fully embrace Christ as our all in all.

The Positive Pathway of Price

The challenge we face in today's world is that we can actually prefer the commonplace pathway of our easy idols. It is the "broad way" of our culture and a difficult thing to relinquish.

That is why we have to turn our eyes on Jesus – so that the things of earth might grow strangely dim. He is our model in all things. Even though He knew all the glories of Heaven and had authority over the riches of this world, He described His lifestyle as one where He did not even have a place to lay His head (Matthew 8:20). No single life has transformed this world more than His, but His impact was completely unrelated to His net worth. It was directly connected to His selfless sacrifice.

In Philippians 3:7-8, Paul shows us how he was walking in the pathway of Christ. Paul counted all reliance on formal learning, social status, and notable accomplishments as "rubbish" or "dung". The idea of "counting as loss" represents an accounting term and reflects a deliberate business transaction that rejects certain assets to gain something more valuable.

Although a brilliant, accomplished, and gifted leader in every respect, Paul always pursued the pathway of price. We read about the detailed losses he faced in 2 Corinthians 11:23-28. This list included a variety of dangers, life-threatening situations, and incredible traumas. This was all a testament of his resolve to be a "servant of Christ" – but in all of these situations, he received abundant grace and was laying up a sure reward in eternity.

Today, you may be facing loss. Consider the example of Paul. Turn your eyes on Jesus. Open your heart to the incalculable "gains" of knowing Christ. No matter what, keep living for the ultimate prize of a life that really matters.

The Great and Growing God – Entertainment

"Little children, keep yourselves from idols."

1 John 5:21

In case you did not notice, Michael Jackson died. His was a sad and tragic story of a hugely famous, immensely talented, and extraordinarily wealthy cultural icon, whose life was very broken and confused. I am sorry for his family and friends who are legitimately grieving his passing.

However, this is not about Michael Jackson. We have all had our fill of the debates about his music, his morality, and the nuances of his personal life. I have no compulsion to weigh in on this. This devotion is about our need to fully grasp this present snapshot of our culture that was captured by the events celebrating Jackson's entertainment legacy.

Desperate for Entertaining Stimulation

The insightful and prophetic writer and pastor A.W. Tozer wrote about our society's captivation with entertainment in a chapter titled, "The Great God Entertainment." His words say it better than mine do:

*". . . the more a man has in his own heart the less he
will require from the outside; excessive need for support
from without is proof of the bankruptcy of the inner*

> *man. . . The present inordinate attachment to every*
> *form of entertainment is evidence that the inner life of*
> *modern man is in serious decline. The average man has*
> *no central core of moral assurance, no spring within*
> *his own breast, no inner strength to place him above*
> *the need for repeated psychological shots to give him*
> *the courage to go on living. He has become a parasite*
> *on the world drawing his life from his environment,*
> *unable to live a day apart from the stimulation which*
> *society affords him."[18]*

He goes on to observe, "There are millions who cannot live without amusement; life without some form of entertainment for them is simply intolerable; they look forward to the blessed relief afforded by professional entertainers and other forms of psychological narcotics as a dope addict looks to his daily shot of heroin. Without them they could not summon courage to face existence."[19]

Tozer's words hardly seem like something written in the mid-50's. Think of what he might observe today in our media dominated, celebrity-crazed, and technology-titillated society. His article would surely become a book of many chapters. Once again, we find ourselves worshiping at the altar of "The Great God Entertainment," cheered on by money-hungry media as we bow in adulation before the latest celebrity icons.

Of course, Tozer quickly adds, as I would, that life is full of legitimate simple pleasures. There is nothing wrong with harmless forms of entertainment that help us relax, stimulate our minds, and enable us to connect with others. We need to find time for good reading, wholesome movies, stimulating hobbies, healthy recreation, and fun with friends and family. If we are burning the candle at both ends we are not as bright as we think we are.

Again, Tozer clarifies, "The all-out devotion to entertainment as a major activity for which and by which men live is definitely something else again. The abuse of a harmless thing is the essence of sin."[20]

So what is the real concern over our abusive interest with entertainment as was so vividly pictured in the media's madness over Jackson's entertainment value in this society?

Entertain me and I will worship you

This almost seems to be the common cry of the empty-souled American. "Worship" may seem a strong word but it is hard to deny the blatant adulation and willing sacrifice of money, time, and attention given to entertainment icons in our culture.

The Apostle Paul warned of these societal trends in 2 Timothy 3, where he wrote, "But know this, that in the last days perilous times will come: For men will be lovers of themselves. . .lovers of pleasure rather than lovers of God."

Tozer again speaks with insight and courage about this very issue when he writes, "It (entertainment) has been built into a multimillion dollar racket with greater power over human minds and human character than any other educational influence on earth. And the ominous thing is that its power is almost exclusively evil, rotting the inner life, crowding out the long eternal thoughts which would fill the souls of men if they were worthy to entertain them. And the whole thing has grown into a veritable religion which holds its devotees with strange fascination, and a religion, incidentally, against which it is now dangerous to speak."[21]

Again, recent news stories show us the incredible influence entertainment holds over swooning fans that faint at the sight of a celebrity and spend exorbitant amounts of money for the latest sound, sight, or sensation dished out by famous and talented entertainers.

True Christ-followers must carefully discern this and resist the lure of excessive and unprofitable entertainment, remembering the first two commandments to worship the Lord God alone and refusing the lure of any kind of idolatry (Exodus 20:3-6). The aged Apostle John appealed to us, "Little children, guard yourselves from idols" (I John 5: 21, NASB).

We should also remember to pray for those we know who are bowing before the god of Entertainment, as we demonstrate the life of Christ and pray for their eyes to be opened to the truth that can fill their souls with life-changing substance and set them free. We also need to pray for those in the entertainment industry to experience an awakening of grace and truth. I am grateful for people like Jim and Karen Covell who have decided to light a candle rather than curse the darkness as they lead the Hollywood Prayer Network, interceding for those in the entertainment industry to turn to Christ (check it out at www. hollywoodprayernetwork.org).

(Part Two)
The Great and Growing God – Entertainment

"We know that we are of God, and the whole world lies under the sway of the wicked one."

1 John 5:19

In Part One of this devotion we recognized that recent events surrounding the death and legacy of Michael Jackson gave us a glimpse of our seeming obsession with entertainment in this nation.

One of the observations we made is that many Americans worship those who entertain them. While "worship" may seem a strong word, it is hard to deny the blatant adulation and willing sacrifice of money, time, and attention given to entertainment icons in our culture.

Many Americans Scorn Those Who Lead Them to Real Worship

The other side of this coin is the reality that many Americans also reject those who call them to true worship. This is not to say that modern-day believers reject the feelings of contemporary songs or the influence of well-known Christian concert artists. This part of our modern-day version of Christianity is "entertaining" and enjoyable. What twenty–first century religious folks don't like is the legitimate and Spirit-filled voices that call them to repent of their idols and bow in absolute surrender and sacrifice before the claims and Lordship of Christ alone. This produces discomfort, and the crowds soon gravitate to an easier, more entertaining feeding source in our land of many spiritual options.

The Apostle Paul's words offer relevant commentary: "For the time will come when they will not endure sound doctrine, but according to their own desires, because they have itching ears, they will heap up for themselves teachers; and they will turn their ears away from the truth, and be turned aside to fables" (2 Timothy 4:2-4 – NKJV).

Our response should be that of Paul's next verse: "But you should keep a clear mind in every situation. Don't be afraid of suffering for the Lord. Work at telling others the Good News, and fully carry out the ministry God has given you" (2 Timothy 4:5, NLT).

Many Christians Have Confused Worship With Entertainment
Our inundation with entertainment and our incorporation thereof into the very fabric of our lives produces a third danger. Again, Tozer says it so very boldly:

> *"For centuries the church stood solidly against every form of worldly entertainment, recognizing it for what it was – a device for wasting time, a refuge from the disturbing voice of conscience, a scheme to divert attention from moral accountability. For this, she got herself abused roundly by the sons of this world. But of late she has become tired of the abuse and has given over the struggle. She appears to have decided that if she cannot conquer the great god Entertainment she may as well join forces with him and make what use she can of his powers. So today we have the astonishing spectacle of millions of dollars being poured in the unholy job of providing earthly entertainment for the so-called sons of heaven. Religious entertainment is in many places rapidly crowding out the serious things*

*of God. Many churches these days have become little
more than poor theatres where fifth-rate 'producers'
peddle their shoddy wares with the full approval of
evangelical leaders who can even quote a holy text in
defense of their delinquency. And hardly a man dares
raise his voice against it."*

In so many ways today we see the symptoms of the slow creep of entertainment into the fabric of our "worship." In many Sunday services
it seems we are more eager to give a standing ovation in response to
human talent than we are to do a face plant in response to the presence of God. Our love for the thrill of visual stimulation seems to
outweigh our hunger for the truth of solid teaching. We can tend to
get more excited about the personality of an amusing speaker than the
challenge brought to our hearts by the clear, uncompromising teaching
of God's Word.

In Philippians 3, Paul spoke about those who polluted real Christian
faith with a reliance on anything else. In his time, it was circumcision. Could entertainment be one of those things in our day? In
Paul's day some proclaimed, "Sure, believe in Jesus – just be circumcised." Today, our cry could be, "Yes, embrace Jesus – but keep it
entertaining."   In the face of this challenge, Paul wrote, "For we are
the true circumcision, who worship God in the Spirit, rejoice in Christ
Jesus, and have no confidence in the flesh."

Today we need a revival of understanding about what it means to
worship God in the Spirit, with or without any of the trappings of
entertaining stimulation. We need a resurgence of joy that is found in
the sufficiency of Jesus Christ, not in the widgets of current worship
trends. We need a resolve to place no confidence in the things of the
flesh or the things designed for the flesh. Our great need is an authentic trust in, and passion for, the truth and presence of Jesus Christ
as the singular centerpiece of our worship – and the source of all our
satisfaction.

Having said all of this, I am very encouraged by what I see in so many places around our nation as pastors and churches are recognizing the failure of an entertainment-oriented approach to truly transform lives. I see a growing desire among church leaders for a fresh focus on the power of genuine worship and a prayerful passion for the transforming presence of Christ experienced in prayer. Even though the idols of entertainment loom large in our culture, the greater power of pure and passionate worship is gripping the hearts of a growing army of gospel-oriented souls, who refuse to bow before any other gods. This is the "renewal army" that will lead the way to a fresh spiritual awakening. By God's grace, I want to be part of that company.

Turning Negative Emotions into Positive Faith

"And without faith it is impossible to please Him..."

Hebrews 11:6 (ESV)

Each one of us on the human journey has experienced some degree of unpleasant and tormenting emotion. Maybe you are in the middle of a storm that has you reeling to find true north in your feelings and thoughts. Many of the great people in the Bible can relate. So can I.

Recently I was struck by the emotional battle but positive breakthrough described in Psalm 22. We know it as a "Messianic Psalm" because it echoes the very words and experiences of Jesus during the darkest moment in human history. He hung on the cross in agony and utter rejection, bearing the full weight of His Father's wrath against our sin. He cried, "My God, My God, why have You forsaken Me?"

Yet, the Psalm was also written as an expression of the real-life distresses of David. We read of his genuine battle to keep faith and embrace hope while grappling with deep anguish and pain. The focus of the Psalm bounces back and forth from descriptions of David's misery to declarations of God's character and ways. This is clear when you see him interrupting his emotional struggle with the repeated declaration of faith, "Yet You, God, are..." (vv. 3, 9 & 19). His emotions swing repeatedly from his real feelings of pain to his faith in his God.

Our Struggle Through Feelings to Embrace Faith

In so many ways, this is a picture of our own struggle to survive and endure the trials of our lives. The battle is not just daily – it is moment by moment. Observe this basic outline of the Psalm that I composed as I have meditated on it in recent days:

> **FEELINGS:** The agony of feeling utterly forsaken – vv. 1-2
> **FAITH:** The truth of God as the holy, reigning God in whom his fathers trusted – vv. 3-5
> **FEELINGS:** The pain of repeated rejection and ridicule – vv. 6-8
> **FAITH:** The truth of God's care and presence in his life since birth – vv. 9-11
> **FEELINGS:** The torment of being threatened and attacked by evil – vv. 12-18
> **FAITH:** The truth of God's present help and deliverance – vv. 19-21

A Breakthrough Perspective

It seems that a breakthrough occurs between vv. 21 & 22. The remainder of the Psalm reflects a restoration of perspective and hope. Here is how it unfolds:

> **LOOKING OUTWARD:** Enlisting others to praise the Lord for His saving help – vv. 22-24
> **LOOKING UPWARD:** Receiving grace for continued praise, obedience, and satisfaction from God – vv. 25-26
> **LOOKING FORWARD:** Declaring God's ultimate victory and the eternal worship of His glorious name – vv. 27-31

Of course, if we go back to the Messianic relevance of the Psalm, we know it is only through the suffering and finished work of Christ in death and resurrection that we can have such a powerful perspective of victory and hope as seen in vv. 22-31. Praise God for the indescribable gift of Christ and His salvation.

Our Choices Today

All of this brings us to the fact of human suffering and the basic set of choices we face every day. Pain, disappointment, fear, and trouble are inevitable in this life. A breakthrough of perspective is optional. I have learned – and have to re-learn every day – that in the midst of trials I must make a choice:

1. Will I believe what I feel, trusting my emotions in the midst of the storm?

2. Will I believe what I see, settling for the temporal problems that surround me?

3. Will I believe what I know to be true about God, keeping my eyes on the eternal reality of who He is and what He will accomplish?

Today, your life may be painful – but God is still holy and faithful. Things may seem out of control – but God is sovereign and wise. The situation you face may feel very unfair – but God is just and righteous in all His ways. Things may appear to be very bad – but God is good and compassionate. You may feel all alone – but God is ever-present and able to comfort your heart. The horizon may seem dark and hopeless – but God is glorious and victorious.

Our emotions are very real, and sometimes troubling. Yet, as David demonstrated in this Psalm, we must keep subjecting what we feel to what we know to be true in order to experience a positive breakthrough in perspective. Jesus also understands our pain and agony. He went from the cruelty of a cross to the darkness of a grave to the glories of Heaven. He lives today, making intercession for us and sympathizing with our weaknesses. He can give us grace to manage our emotions and live in dynamic faith today. Yes, it is a battle – but it is a battle that has been won, and can be won, through Christ.

Do it Today!

"Do whatever he tells you."

John 2:5 (ESV)

Felix, the Roman procurator of Judea, lived by the motto "tomorrow." Paul boldly proclaimed the Gospel to this powerful official. Acts says, "As he reasoned with them about righteousness and self-control and the judgment to come, Felix was terrified. 'Go away for now,' he replied. 'When it is more convenient, I'll call for you again.'" His response was a tragic "tomorrow." It must not be ours.

You see, "tomorrow" is not just the Devil's favorite word for those considering salvation, but it is a favorite tactic against every believer seeking to follow Christ. I was reminded of this recently when I read Hebrews 3:1-15:

"Therefore, holy brethren, partakers of the heavenly calling, consider the Apostle and High Priest of our confession, Christ Jesus, who was faithful to Him who appointed Him...Therefore, as the Holy Spirit says:

"Today, if you will hear His voice,
Do not harden your hearts as in the rebellion,
In the day of trial in the wilderness,
Where your fathers tested Me, tried Me,

And saw My works forty years.
Therefore I was angry with that generation,
And said, 'They always go astray in their heart,
And they have not known My ways.'
So I swore in My wrath,
'They shall not enter My rest.'"

Without sermonizing, let me simply offer a few observations from this text.

- It is today that God calls us to hear his voice and not harden our hearts.

- Our failure to obey His voice today results in a hardening of our hearts toward God.

- God considers today's hardened heart a spirit of rebellion.

- There is strong sense of God's displeasure when we harden our hearts today while forgetting His faithfulness and provision of yesterday.

- A hardened heart today will often result in the Father's chastisement tomorrow.

- Today we must be on full alert as we avoid an evil heart of unbelief.
- Today the deceitfulness of sin comes against us, encouraging us to develop a philosophy of "tomorrow-ism."

Let us pray for one another today. God's call is often costly, but it is always good and always rewarding. Is the Lord calling you to serve His church, to reconcile with another, to give generously to His kingdom, to share Christ with a neighbor and to love your spouse more intentionally and sacrificially?

Remember the words of Mary as she spoke to the servants at the wedding ceremony in John 2:5. She said to the servants, "Do whatever he tells you." When the God of this universe speaks, may we ever avoid the tragedy of Felix, and never respond like this: "Go away for now. When it is more convenient, I'll call for you again." Today, may we hear His voice and obey.

Walking With Our Creator God

"For He knows our frame; He remembers that we are dust."

Psalm 103:14 (ESV)

As we walk with our Creator God, becoming like him means exercising this attribute He has given us. Thus, our prayer lives should be filled with creativity, innovation and spontaneity.

We must remember that God is not the author of boredom, especially when we are conversing with Him. He is not the author of lethargy, apathy, despondency or defeat. At the beginning of each day, each new year and every endeavor, we begin again in life with the very presence of the Creator God in our hearts.

He created the magnificence of this universe (which man has not even begun to comprehend)! Certainly, He can "do exceedingly abundantly above all that we ask or think, according to the power that works in us" (Ephesians 3:20). Through the finished work of Christ, we are now reconciled to the Creator, and His very presence is within us by the Holy Spirit. So what are the blessings of knowing and trusting the Creator?

New Creatures

First, we can live as new creatures in Christ! 2 Corinthians 5:16-17 says, "Therefore, from now on, we regard no one according to the flesh. Even though we have known Christ according to the flesh, yet now we know Him thus no longer. Therefore, if anyone is in Christ, he is a new creation; old things have passed away; behold, all things have become new."

By the power of His salvation, we are new people. We now live in Christ. We do not see people or life through the old, stale lenses of the flesh. Literally all things are becoming new every day. As the Amplified Bible puts it, "The fresh and new has come!" That is the joy of living with the presence of the Creator in us.

New Hearts

Second, we can experience renewed hearts! Even after all his failures, lies and hard-heartedness, David was able to look to his Creator and pray, "Create in me a clean heart, O God, and renew a steadfast spirit within me" (Psalm 51:10). Regardless of the regret and pain you are carrying with you now, you can express this same trust in the One who makes all things new. He is a heart specialist, or, as another man has put it, "God is good with a mop." He can clean up all the shame, regret, guilt and condemnation through the power of confession (1 John 1:9), and he can renew a steadfast, loyal and persevering spirit within us.

New Beginnings

Third, we can enjoy the praise of a restored life! In Isaiah 57:19, the Lord spoke of His future restoration of Israel with these words: "Peace, peace, to him who is far off [both Jew and Gentile] and to him who is near, says the Lord; I create the fruit of his lips, and I will heal him and make his lips blossom anew with speech in thankful praise" (AMP). At the dawn of each new day, God can produce a powerful supernatural peace in your heart. He can take your words of doubt, complaint and discontent, and replace them with newly created praise as you allow Him to heal your heart. Let the Creator restore his work as you humble yourself before Him, trusting Him for a fresh touch of His grace (see Isaiah 57:15).

New Relationships

Fourth, we can rediscover the power of reconciliation! A powerful dimension of His creative power is seen in the reality of the body of Christ. Ephesians 2:15 tells us that Christ has ". . . created in Himself one new man from the two, thus making peace." The normal state for those in Christ is oneness, unity, reconciliation, grace and forgiveness. You cannot achieve these by your own resolve or self-effort. But the Creator is at work all around the world today, breaking down the walls of sinful separation and making people "one" by His grace.

New Insights

Fifth, we anticipate fresh spiritual insight and experience! In recent months, I have fallen in love with the truth of 1 Corinthians 2:9-12: "But as it is written: Eye has not seen, nor ear heard, nor have entered into the heart of man the things which God has prepared for those who love Him. But God has revealed them to us through His Spirit . . . Now we have received, not the spirit of the world, but the Spirit who is from God, that we might know the things that have been freely given to us by God." Let the Creator create in you a fresh perspective every day as His Spirit illumines His Word and fills your life with ever-new insights. There is nothing stale about life with Christ when we understand that "In the beginning God created...." He continues to make all things new for us every day.

Father, help us to live with grand expectations as we look to You as our Creator and watch expectantly as You unfold Your plan for our hearts, homes and churches through the power of Your Spirit within us.

A Healthy Reaction to Trouble

"These things I have spoken to you, that in Me you may have peace. In the world you will have tribulation; but be of good cheer, I have overcome the world."

John 16:33

Good Christians are always in trouble — not with the law, but with the devil and his loyalists. Sometimes our God, who is more interested in our character than our comfort, allows troubles of a different kind in order to make us more effective and exemplary in our Christward journey.

The early Christians were facing constant trouble. It came in the form of persecution (Acts 4), corruption (Acts 5), potential division (Acts 6:2) and pressing distractions (Acts 6:2-4). They were praying menaces to the kingdom of darkness, and the ruler of this dark kingdom was on constant counterattack.

If we are going to follow Christ with a serious dedication, we too will encounter many troubles. It is a promise (2 Timothy 3:12). The question is not IF we will go through difficult times, but *how* we will react to them.

I remember reading a chapter by Watchman Nee many years ago where he wrote on "The Christian Reaction." He concluded that we can tell a lot more about a Christian by his reactions than by his actions. Actions can be calculated and manipulated. Reactions tend to come straight from the gut and expose the nature of our soul.

In studying Acts 4:23-31, I am impressed and helped by the reaction of the early Christ followers. Their leaders, Peter and John, were sequestered, questioned and threatened with a warning to stop preaching the Gospel. In Acts 4:23 they went back to the gathered Christians and reported on the trouble they had seen. Then the text says in v. 24, "So when they heard that...." Stop. Read carefully here.

But before you do, ask yourself a few questions. How do I respond to bad news? What do I feel when someone I love has been maligned or mistreated? When my safety is shaken or even when my life is threatened, what do I say? How do I respond to unanticipated and painful difficulties in my life? Think about your answers honestly and candidly before proceeding.

Now, let's glean some inspiration from these early believers. The account goes on to say, "So when they heard that, they raised their voice to God with one accord and said: 'Lord, You are God, who made heaven and earth and the sea, and all that is in them . . .'" (v. 24). They did not picket, send nasty e-mails, appeal to Caesar or grumble among themselves. They worshiped God!

Reaction One: Worshiping God for Who He Is

When in trouble, worship should not be our last resort, but our first response. In my first book, *The 7 Most Important Questions You'll Ever Answer*, I noted that the most important question in every life is, "Who is God?" This is especially true in times of trouble.

When facing difficulties, we tend to ask questions like, "Why is this happening?" or "What did I do to deserve this? " or "Now what is going to happen with my life and my plans?" Instead – and instinctively – these believers went back to the foundational issue. They worshiped God.

In this passage, they proclaimed God's character with united hearts and voices (a strong statement about the need to stay and pray in community when you face problems). They extolled Him as the Lord, the Sovereign God, the Creator and Controller of all things, the One whose Word is true and reliable. They acknowledged that these difficult experiences were clearly within the scope of God's plan. They knew that all of human history, and their histories, centered in Jesus.

When we encounter overwhelming trouble, it is important to remember the reassurance of Scripture. Isaiah 26:3 says this: "You will keep him in perfect peace, whose mind is stayed on You, because he trusts in You." Consider Daniel 11:32, which says, ". . . but the people who know their God shall be strong, and carry out great exploits." These promises were on practical display in Acts 4. They worked for these early Christians, and they will work for us as we allow them to regulate our thoughts and emotions.

Reaction Two: Seeing Ourselves for Who We Are

In a modern world where so many people react to trouble by claiming their rights in an aggressive display of ego or in coddling their fears in a fit of depression, these early Christians are a refreshing contrast. Having embraced a solid picture of God, they went on to declare the truth about themselves. Verse 29 says, "Now, Lord, look on their threats, and grant to Your servants...."

Servants. That's how they saw themselves. Servants have no rights, only the honor of accomplishing the agenda of the one to whom they are subject. Trouble has a way of revealing our true view of our place in this world. I remember Gordon MacDonald saying, "Everyone wants to be a servant until someone treats them like one." Problems and pain test our commitment to servanthood.

Our identity in Christ is a powerful and fundamental truth for surviving tough times. Remembering that we are beloved, accepted, righteous and complete in Christ gives us real security. Recalling that we are members of His body, the light of the world, the salt of the earth, ambassadors and slaves keeps our focus on something other than ourselves.

Reaction Three: Embracing Our Purpose in His Power

As I have reviewed this story over and over, my personal summary of this account is, "When trouble comes, it's not about us. It's about Jesus – His name, His fame and His claim on our lives. Trouble is a fresh call to stay on task and remain faithful to His mission."

Acts 4:29-31 describes it this way, "'Now, Lord, look on their threats, and grant to Your servants that with all boldness they may speak Your word, by stretching out Your hand to heal, and that signs and wonders may be done through the name of Your holy Servant Jesus.' And when they had prayed, the place where they were assembled together was shaken; and they were all filled with the Holy Spirit, and they spoke the word of God with boldness."

It is notable to see how willing God was to take control of these yielded hearts and lives by His Spirit. Again, this picture of the central role of the Holy Spirit reminds us that we don't ultimately endure troubled times by our own strength and resolve. In spite of how we might feel, we have to make the right choices, open our hearts to the right truth and submit to His available power.

The Three Most Important Questions

Years ago as the Lord began to inspire my heart with the "Seven Questions" renewal process, I concluded that the first three questions we must answer from the truth of God's Word are these:

- Who is God?
- Who am I?
- Why am I here?

I find it fascinating that these early Christians seemed to come back to this vital focus during a very threatening moment. As we affirm our answers to these questions and rehearse them daily, we will be ready for disappointments, dilemmas and difficulties.

If you are not in trouble today, it will probably find you tomorrow. Be ready, and choose well. You will become better, not bitter. Your life will be more fruitful and less frustrated. Faith will replace fear. A healthy reaction will result in a hopeful and impactful life.

The Gospel According to Twitter

"Take heed that you do not tweet your charitable deeds before men, to be seen by them."

"Take heed that you do not tweet your charitable deeds before men, to be seen by them. Otherwise you have no reward from your Father in heaven."

Introduction to the Epistle of First Twitter

First Twitter, written in 2009 by Pastor Daniel Henderson, is not inspired Scripture, although the author borrows heavily from the Bible. Penned from seat 4B at 25,000 feet during a recent Delta Airlines flight, the epistle is short and eclectic, reflecting many familiar biblical themes. The purpose of the book is to evoke fresh, heartfelt evaluation of the growing social networking tool known as Twitter.

The author acknowledges that Twitter is a very positive and powerful means for sharing updates and prayer requests. He claims no particular expertise on the subject but expresses a concern for pure motives and Christ-honoring messages among the current barrage of "tweets." Since its creation, the epistle has not seen widespread circulation. The author simply wrote it with the intent of creating a tool to evaluate his own heart and helping others do the same.

Special Concerns about the Epistle

As you read this short epistle it is important that the application remain personal and not serve as a means by which to judge the tweets of others. As one verse in the epistle says, "Therefore judge no tweets before the time, until the Lord comes, who will both bring to light the hidden things of darkness and reveal the counsels of the hearts. Then each one's praise will come from God."

Interpretive Guidelines

Theologians and critics (including only Henderson so far) who have evaluated this somewhat controversial epistle offer the following questions as a guideline for interpreting and applying the message of the Epistle of First Twitter:

- What messages are my tweets conveying?
- Why do I want to convey them?
- What impact will they have?
- What praise or reward am I seeking?

Finally, for those unfamiliar with the terms used in this epistle, we offer the following:

- **Twitter** = A social networking tool to keep family, friends, and coworkers up-to-date on what an individual is doing by using an instant messenger service, the Web, as well as mobile texting, plus other venues. Messages are limited to 140 characters, which is just enough for a quick update.
- **Tweet** = a short message sent on Twitter.
- **RT** = a "re-tweet," when someone reposts a tweet sent by another person, passing it on to their followers as well.
- **Twitpic** = a photograph of a person or event that is attached to a tweet and sent to followers.

The Book of First Twitter

Tweetverbs for Today

Do not send boastful tweets about tomorrow, for you do not know what a day may bring forth. Let another man praise you, and not your own tweets; a stranger, and not your own mobile device. (Adapted from Proverbs 27:1-2)

Every tweet of a man is right in his own eyes, but the LORD weighs the hearts. (Adapted from Proverbs 21:2)

Twitter on the Mount

Take heed that you do not tweet your charitable deeds before men, to be seen by them. Otherwise you have no reward from your Father in heaven. Therefore, when you do a charitable deed, do not tweet to all of your followers as the hypocrites do in the synagogues and in the streets, that they may have glory from men. Assuredly, I say to you, they have their reward. But when you do a charitable deed, do not let your left hand know what your right hand is doing, that your charitable deed may be in secret; and your Father who sees in secret will Himself reward you openly.

And when you pray, you shall not be like the hypocrites. For they love to tweet their prayers to all of their followers that they may be seen by men. Assuredly, I say to you, they have their reward. But you, when you pray, send a private text message to your friend as you pray to your Father who is in the secret place; and your Father who sees in secret will reward you openly. (Adapted from Matthew 6:1-6)

The Pastor and the Backslider

Two men picked up their mobile devices to tweet, one a pastor and the other a backslidden Baptist. The pastor composed a message and wrote thus with himself: "Praise God that I am not like other men — boring, inarticulate, and not well-traveled or even as this backslider. I post twitpics twice a day; I give blessings to all those who follow me." And the backslider, hardly able to type, would not so much as post a pic, but trembled as he held his Blackberry, saying, "God, be merciful to me, a boring person." I tell you, this man went down to his office justified rather than the other; for everyone who exalts himself will be humbled, and he who humbles himself will be exalted. (Adapted from Luke 18:10-14)

Rewards

But he is a Christian who is one inwardly; with messages that remain of the heart, in the Spirit, not in the Twitter world; whose praise is not from men but from God. (Adapted from Romans 2:29)

For we are God's fellow social networkers; you are God's followers (and ours), you are God's network. According to the grace of God which was given to me, as a wise social networker I have birthed the idea, and another comments on it. But let each one take heed how he comments. For no other foundation can anyone lay than that which is laid, which is Jesus Christ. Now if anyone responds to my tweets, it may be gold, silver, precious stones, wood, hay, straw – each one's tweets will become clear; for the Day will declare it, because it will be revealed by fire; and the fire will test each one's content, of what sort it is. If anyone's tweets endure, he will receive a reward. If anyone's tweets are burned, he will suffer loss; but he himself will be saved, yet so as through fire. (Adapted from 1 Corinthians 3:9-15)

Do Not Judge

But with me it is a very small thing that I should be judged by you or by any social network. In fact, I do not even judge myself. For I know of nothing against myself, yet I am not justified by this; but He who judges me is the Lord. Therefore judge no tweets before the time, until the Lord comes, who will both bring to light the hidden things of darkness and reveal the counsels of the hearts. Then each one's praise will come from God. (Adapted from 1 Corinthians 4:3-5)

Comparing and Commending

Do we begin again to commend ourselves on Twitter? Or do we need, as some others, RT's of commendation to you or RT's of commendation from you? You are our epistle written in our hearts, known and read by all men; clearly you are an epistle of Christ, ministered to by us, created not by tweets but by the Spirit of the living God, not on screens of mobile devices but on tablets of flesh, that is, of the heart. (Adapted from 2 Corinthians 3:1-3)

For we dare not count our Twitter followers or compare ourselves with those who commend themselves. But they, measuring themselves by themselves, and comparing themselves among themselves, are not wise. But "he who glories, let him glory in the LORD." For not he who commends himself is approved, but he whom the Lord commends. (Adapted from 2 Corinthians 10:12 & 18)

On Prayer

"Prayerlessness is our declaration of independence from God."

Power in Praying the Scriptures

"The testimony of the Lord is sure, making wise the simple."

Psalm 19:7 (ESV)

By conviction and experience I have concluded that the most creative and powerful prayers spring from the inexhaustible treasury of the word of God. Thousands of times I have watched the Bible expose hearts, guide language, unite diverse interests and create powerful moments of remarkable prayer.

Biblical Vocabulary

Eugene Peterson said it well: "Prayer is language used to respond to the most that has been said to us with the potential for saying all that is in us... Prayer is dangerous...it moves our language into potencies we are unaccustomed to and unprepared for...We restore prayer to its context in God's word. Prayer is not something we think up to get God's attention or enlist his favor. Prayer is answering speech. The first word is God's word. Prayer is a human word and is never the first word, never the primary word, never the initiating and shaping word simply because we are never first; never primary . . . the first word everywhere and always is God's word to us, not ours to him."

Peterson's insights remind me of a lesson I've learned over the years about the value of letting the Bible shape the vocabulary of prayer. It's sad, but somewhat humorous, to observe what happens in a prayer time that is based on stale human vocabulary rather than God's word.

Have you been to one of those prayer times where some verbose participant blurts out a protracted prayer-speech using some cheap imitation of King James English? They even sometimes change the tone of their voice to sound more holy.

After ten minutes of this oratory, the efforts finally conclude. What usually follows is unresponsive silence. The prayer meeting is dead on arrival. Most people are thinking, "Wow, how can I follow a prayer like that? I just talk like a normal person. Will God hear my simple prayer after that masterpiece?" Someone else may be thinking, "What in the world did that guy just say? How do I pray in agreement with that? I didn't even understand it!"

Common Ground

Finding our language in Scripture allows everyone to discover an entry point. The Bible provides handles for mature saints and struggling ones too. It is a wonderful thing to observe this dynamic. This is at the heart of teaching people how to effectivly pray.

Recently, a dear friend pulled me aside to say thank you for the power of this emphasis. She essentially said, "I never realized how simple but meaningful this kind of prayer can be. I've been in attendance each morning and tried to sit in several parts of the room so that I can pray with different people. Yesterday, I was in a small group with four men. Each responded so sincerely as they prayed the scripture. It moved me to the point that I wanted to place my hand on each one just to let them know I understood and agreed with them in prayer. It was so very moving. The Spirit was really at work, and I love learning how to pray straight from the Bible."

Jonathan Edwards wrote, "The Spirit who causes men to have greater regard for the Holy Scriptures and establishes them more in their truth and divine inspiration is certainly the Spirit of God. . . It is this word that God has given to be the great standing rule for the direction of His church in all spiritual matters and for all concerns of their souls in all ages. A spirit of delusion will not incline persons to seek direction from the mouth of God."[22]

What a focus! This is the central passion of real prayer. May we always seek our direction in prayer from The mouth of God as we pray with opened Bibles.

Prayer and the Peace of God

"Let the peace of God rule in your hearts."

Colossians 3:15

On several occasions in recent days, I've had the opportunity to study and preach from Romans 15:30-33. In this passage, Paul urges the believers in the church at Rome to gather together with a passionate regard for the Lord Jesus and a love for the person and work of the Holy Spirit. He pleads with them to pray intensely, literally agonize for the work of the gospel, and then for him personally.

Paul first asks the Romans to intercede for his protection from the enemies of the gospel, for the prosperity of his ministry within the church, and for God's provision for his own personal refreshment. Then, he adds this profound blessing: "Now the God of Peace be with you all."

It seems a bit strange that peace should come from agonizing prayer, but this is the way of God. In a less intense context, Paul gave us this admonition: "Be anxious for nothing, but in everything by prayer and supplication, with thanksgiving, let your requests be made known to God; and the peace of God, which surpasses all understanding, will guard your hearts and minds through Christ Jesus" (Philippians 4:6-7). Paul faced constant attack, antagonism and anxiety. As long as we live in this fallen world we will experience the same troubles. The question is not if these things will come upon us, but how we will respond. Will we fall to our knees? Or will we stand in our own strength, figure it out independently and ultimately falter?

What is this connection between prayer and peace? Through prayer, the Lord neutralizes confusion, resulting in peace. Through prayer, the Lord provides contentment and comfort, enriching our peace. Through prayer, the Lord brings conformity unto godliness, promoting true peace. And through prayer, we have the comfort of the Lord's presence, which is our source of peace.

Scripture is full and rich in this assurance. As you read through these verses, ask the Lord to reveal His truth about prayer and peace:

- "Finally brethren, farewell. Become complete. Be of good comfort, be of one mind, live in peace; and the God of love and peace will be with you" (2 Corinthians 13:11).

- "The things which you learned and received and heard and saw in me, these do, and the God of peace will be with you" (Philippians 4:9).

- "Now may the Lord of peace Himself give you peace always in every way. The Lord be with you all" (2 Thessalonians 3:16).

- "Now may the God of peace who brought up our Lord Jesus from the dead, that great Shepherd of the sheep, through the blood of the everlasting covenant, make you complete in every good work to do His will, working in you what is well pleasing in His sight, through Jesus Christ, to whom be glory forever and ever. Amen"
(Hebrews 13:20-21).

- "For God is not the author of confusion but of peace, as in all the churches of the saints" (1 Corinthians 14:33).

Seek, Don't Speak

"My flesh and my heart fail; But God is the strength of my heart and my portion forever."

Psalm 73:26

Asaph, the author of Psalm 73, was Israel's chief musician and worship leader. In Psalm 73, Asaph reflected on the goodness of God. He journaled about a season of deep spiritual struggle. He compared the plight of the godly with the apparent prosperity and ease of the ungodly. He explained that something occurs when he returns to the sanctuary of God for fresh perspective. He followed this with deep repentance and a full restoration of His joy and sufficiency in the Lord.

But just before he experienced the breakthrough, he made an intriguing but powerful statement. In verse 15 he said, "Had I spoken thus [given expression to my feelings], I would have been untrue and have dealt treacherously against the generation of Your children" (AMP).

Like Asaph, we all go through struggles, regrets, personal grievances and subjective critical judgments. Asaph rejoices that he had the spiritual sense and self-control to guard his tongue. A failure to do so would have been a betrayal—an act of treachery and a pillaging of God's people. He recognized the serious nature of an undiscerning emotional spew.

Asaph took a right turn into the sanctuary. It is here that he experienced a powerful attitude adjustment, leading to repentance and restoration. Sadly, many troubled believers take a left turn into the muck of complaining and gossip, often resulting in "treachery" against God's people, the church.

Here is a crucial crossroads for every one of us. We know the tongue is a destructive fire. Death and life are in the power of the tongue (James 3:6, Proverbs 18:21). We will be held accountable for every idle word (Matthew 12:36). Paul urges us to restrict our words to those expressions that build and bless (Ephesians 4:29).

The wisdom of Asaph is clear and is worth our utmost consideration. Next time you are absorbed in negativity, seek. Don't speak. Hold your tongue, and honor the Lord with your humility.

Helping Your Church Win by Helping Your Pastor Win

"Let them do so with joy and not with grief, for that would be unprofitablefor you."

Hebrews 13:17

In a recent interview with Leith Anderson, a pastoral colleague and President of the National Association of Evangelicals, he made a statement that I've not been able to shake. He said, "Churches do more to help pastors succeed than pastors do to help churches succeed."

In a culture that tends to idolize the ideal leader, it seems we've lost our way as it relates to the proper relationship between shepherds and sheep. Much could be said about the responsibilities of the shepherd, but I will at least say this: the call to true integrity must sound loud today in a society that defines "leaders" by their appearance, smile, hairstyle and entertainment quotient. A passion for the truth must be cultivated anew in the face of many temptations pastors face everyday.

However, let's focus on the sheep for a moment (particularly, the sheep that bite and the sheep that misbehave). These sheep keep shepherds so distracted with their wanderings that the shepherd loses the energy to care for himself, let alone the many other legitimate needs of the flock.

In a recent gathering at a local church, someone asked, "What can people do to support their leaders?" With no script or outline, I simply answered from my heart with three convictions. Maybe they will help you as well:

Stop the comparisons!

I often say that comparison is an ugly game. No one ever wins! If you are compared favorably, it results in pride. If you are compared unfavorably, it results in self-doubt and even self-pity. Current pastors are often compared to the previous pastors or to other "successful" clergy across town. In the same interview, Leith Anderson noted, "Fifty years ago, the only way someone would compare their pastor with another is when they went on vacation. Today, because of radio teachers, TV preachers and authors galore, pastors are compared everyday to an unrealistic and unfair standard." It is true. And it is unnecessary, unhealthy and debilitating. Discontented sheep are formed by unrealistic standards and unfair comparisons. If God is sovereign (and He is!), it is your duty to support the one God has placed as the leader of your church.

Guard your tongue!

The tongue is a fire. In some cases it is a flamethrower, and in other cases it is just an initiating spark. In every case, it has the potential to destroy. Proverbs says, "Death and life are in the power of the tongue" (18:21). Many years ago, I sat in with my friend Al Broom, former Executive Pastor of First Baptist Church of Modesto, California. He offered profound insight when he said, "The number one problem of the local church is the toleration of known sin." He then added, "The number one sin of the church is a critical spirit." A critical spirit is very often at the source of caustic and condemning speech. When it is targeted at pastors, it is especially damaging to the health of a congregation.

Stay on your knees!

Of course, it is nearly impossible to be a sincere intercessor and a critic at the same time. Prayer can stop a negative tongue and unleash a positive movement of support. The truth is that every pastor desperately needs the prayer of God's people. The Apostle Paul was bold in his requests for supportive prayer (2 Corinthians 1:8-11, Ephesians 6:18-19, Colossians 4:2-4, 1 Thessalonians 5:25, and 2 Thessalon-ians 3:1).

I like to remind Christians that if they are not happy with their pastor, they should not criticize him. Pray for him! And pray for your own spirit while you're at it! Those saints who think the pastor is supposed to make the church succeed but who are not entirely determined to make their pastor succeed suffer from myopia and strategic confusion. No church can succeed without stable leadership. No leader can truly succeed without determined and supportive people.

The most strategic investment you can make for your church is your sincere intercession on your pastor's behalf. Help your church win by overtly and enthusiastically helping your pastor win. The Kingdom of God will advance, the community will be blessed, and Jesus Christ will be honored.

The Greatest Gift

"Now I beg you, brethren, through the Lord Jesus Christ, and through the love of the Spirit, that you strive together with me in prayers to God for me."

Romans 15:30

There are many common tangible expressions of appreciation to give your pastor or spiritual leaders. Yet the most important demonstration of your love is intangible. In the economy of God's ways, this demonstration is a gift of numerous profound and substantial blessings.

Charles Spurgeon felt his people could show him no greater kindness than to pray for him Paul repeatedly expressed this same desire and appealed to the New Testament congregations. But why is prayer such an important and loving gift? What difference does it really make?

Enjoying the Benefits

Romans 15:30-33 states that the prayers of God's people are powerful in the protection of God's servants as they encounter the enemies of the Gospel. Prayer enables the prosperity and blessing of ministry within the church. According to this passage, prayer is also a vital ingredient in the refreshment of the heart and soul of a leader.

And there are other profound benefits. Often we don't know when our spiritual leaders are in trouble emotionally, physically, spiritually or socially. In 2 Corinthians 1:8-11, Paul reflected on a very difficult time in his ministry when he was "burdened beyond measure, above strength," so much so that he "despaired even of life" and felt he had a "sentence of death" on his life. He notes that faithful prayer was a vital element in his survival through this difficult time. He also explained that because God's people prayed, a great sense of thanksgiving rose to God.

Ephesians 6:18-19 presents prayer for spiritual leaders as a strategic and powerful weapon in the context of spiritual warfare. According to this passage, our prayers for help empower Christ's servants to speak the truth clearly and boldly. In Colossians 4:2-4, Paul reiterates the vital role of prayer in the effectiveness of his preaching and teaching. He notes that prayer is even vital in opening the right doors of opportunity for effective ministry.

In 1 Thessalonians 5:25 Paul simply pleads, "Brethren, pray for us." In his next letter to the Thessalonians, he elaborates by writing, "Finally, brethren, pray for us, that the word of the Lord may run swiftly and be glorified, just as it is with you, and that we may be delivered from unreasonable and wicked men; for not all have faith" (2 Thessalonians 3:1-2). What a powerful impact our prayers can have in enabling the truth to spread and amplify God's glory in the world.

In these requests, we should also notice the plural pronoun us. The great benefit of our prayers goes beyond a single leader. They touch the ministry team, the pastoral family and others who serve alongside our spiritual leaders.

Praying for God's Best

If we are content with powerless ministry, ineffective preaching, fallen pastors, broken ministry families, congregational discord and burned out leaders, then we do not need to expend our best efforts in prayer. However, if we want to see God's power and goodness in our lives and churches, we must pray.

We all want this and realize that our churches desperately need these blessings. The greatest gift you can give spiritual leaders cannot be purchased at the Christian bookstore or be contained in a gift card. It flows down from the throne of grace in response to the passionate and humble cry of God's people. Your prayers are truly the supernatural gift that keeps giving, for Christ's glory and the benefit of countless others. There is no limit to the benefit of this gift. As you consider the battles we face in today's culture, give generously by interceding on behalf of those who are called to shepherd the church of Jesus Christ.

The Enduring Motivation for Prayer

"You are worthy, O Lord, to recieve glory and honor and power..."

Revelation 4:11

All believers know that we *should* pray. Some know *how* to pray. Ultimately, we must understand *why* we pray. While duty and ability can be valuable to our prayer lives, our greatest need is an enduring motivation that fuels consistent passion in our pursuit of God and His purposes through prayer.

Skeptic philosopher Friedrich Nietzsche believed, he who has a why to live can bear almost any how. I remember hearing publisher and author Charles "Tremendous" Jones say that if you teach someone how to do something, they will persist for a while. If you teach them why they are doing it, it will take a brick wall to stop them.

Some months ago, I was asked by a prominent Christian leader why I was so passionate about prayer. He asked, "Is it something about the family you were raised in?" I laughed. First, I do not feel that my commitment is really that great compared to the biblical standard. Secondly, while I knew it had nothing to do with my family, I really had not analyzed the components of all that motivates me. As a result, I sat down and wrote out the factors that seem to spark my own heart toward a life of enduring prayer. Perhaps these elements will help you.

Five Biblical Motivations for a Life of Enduring Prayer

1. The Priorities of Spiritual Leadership
As a pastor, my heart is always challenged by the biblical models of prayer. In both the Old and New Testaments, I discovered very clear examples of the core priorities of spiritual leaders.

In the Old Testament, we remember the leadership crisis Moses faced when he was overwhelmed from judging too many of the people of Israel. Jethro, his wise father-in-law, advised him to focus his energies on the things that mattered most. Read his advice carefully: "Listen now to my voice; I will give you counsel, and God will be with you: Stand before God for the people, so that you may bring the difficulties to God. And you shall teach them the statutes and the laws, and show them the way in which they must walk and the work they must do. Moreover you shall select from all the people able men . . . And let them judge the people at all times" (Exodus 18:19-22). Did you catch the three priorities? They are prayer, the word, and delegation.

Similarly, in the New Testament, we see the salient example of a leadership crisis in Acts 6:1-7. Verse 4 clearly describes the priorities of the apostles: "...but we will give ourselves continually to prayer and to the ministry of the word." Again, in this context, the three priorities are prayer, the word, and delegation. The apostles assigned seven men to handle the feeding of the widows so they could continue in prayer and the Word.

It is pretty clear. Both Testaments present a mirror image of prayer, the word, and delegation. This motivates me to align my life with the biblical standard. The cultural standard of modern-day church models presents many other alternatives like planning, strategy, organization, administration, creative communication, high-tech services, small-groups, counseling, age-specific programming, attractive activities, and a whole array of other "priorities." Many of these are good — but enemies of the best. So every Christian leader must decide on the pattern he will use to set his priorities and motivations for ministry. I think the biblical record is quite clear – and I try to stay motivated accordingly.

2. The Persuasion of New Testament Christianity

The model of New Testament believers is also a clear example that motivates us. We all know that everything the early church did was rooted, bathed, and empowered in prayer. Real, united, passionate prayer was not the only thing they did – it was just the first thing they did. As a result, the church was begun out of prayer, grown by prayer, enlivened in prayer, guided through prayer, delivered by prayer, and launched in Holy Spirit power into a needy world via prayer (Acts 1:13-14, 24; 2:42; 3:1; 4:24-31; 6:4; 9:4; 10:9; 12:5, 12;13:1-3; etc.). They turned the world upside down without any of the tools and resources we have at our disposal. Yet they knew the power of God through intimate, united connection with Him. Prayer was their tool of choice, and that can motivate us to try to make it our choice in spite of the many distractions of this busy, high-tech world in which we live.

3. The Pattern of Jesus' Prayer Life

Jesus was fully God and fully man. This is the mystery of the "kenosis" (Greek for "emptiness") for theologians and new believers alike. As God, He was in constant perfect communion with the Father and did not need to pray in the sense that we do. Yet, as fully man, he carried out the perfect example of humble, constant, passionate communion with the Father (see Luke 5:16; 6:12; 9:18, 28-29; 11:1; 22:39; Mark 1:35;6:46; Matthew 17:21). If he demonstrated prayer in such a clear and passionate fashion, how much more should we be motivated to pray in our fallen condition?

4. The Passion for an Eternally Significant Life

Consider this definition of prayer: "Intimacy with God that leads to the fulfillment of His purposes, accomplished by His power, for His glory." Ministry that does not spring from intimacy is merely activity without the touch of eternity. Jesus made it clear that enduring fruit must spring from an abiding reliance on Him (John 15:1-8). Matthew

7:21-23 is a riveting reminder that even high-impact preaching and deliverance ministry that does not spring from authentic intimacy will be completely disregarded in eternity. 1 Corinthians 3:9-15 also reminds us that our Christian life and service will be either wood, hay, and stubble or enduring gold, silver, and precious stones, depending on the "sort" (not the size) of what we have done.

I could tell countless stories of pastors I have met who have come to the realization that Acts 1 must come before Acts 2 in order to have a prayerful, Spirit-empowered, and eternally significant ministry. As I've noted before, "Our greatest fear is not that we fail but that we succeed in things that do not matter." A genuine life of prayer brings eternal wisdom, power, and value to all that we do. That is motivating.

5. The Pursuit of the Worthiness / Neediness Attitude

I've said so often, "The only enduring motive for prayer is that God is worthy to be sought." This is so motivating, and it is the heart of worship-based prayer. It is the focus of seeking His face (person), not just His hand (provision). It is the focus on the relationship we desire with Him, not just the resources we think we need from Him. The only form of prayer that will last for eternity is worshipful prayer – there will be no more requests, spiritual warfare, or need to surrender the will of our flesh – just pure, glorious worship.

The flip side of saying, "He is worthy" is to confess that "I am needy." His worthiness and my weakness are powerful motivators to pray – even when I do not feel like it or find it inconvenient.

In His powerful appearance and message to the lukewarm church of Laodicea, Jesus motivates their worship of Him by describing Himself as "the Amen, the Faithful and True Witness, the Beginning of the creation of God." Then He compels them to recognize their weaknesses by stating, "...you say, 'I am rich, have become wealthy, and have need of nothing' — and do not know that you are wretched, miserable, poor, blind, and naked...." His worthiness and our neediness are vital to enduring prayer.

Our Response to this Motivational Call?

With these motivations in mind, how should we respond? Perhaps Jesus' final words to the Laodicean believers provide the perfect conclusion. He writes, "Therefore be zealous and repent. Behold, I stand at the door and knock. If anyone hears My voice and opens the door, I will come in to him and dine with him, and he with Me."

Accordingly, we can repent of our weak and wavering motivations. We can hear Him knocking on our heart's door, inviting us to journey deeper in our motivations and closer in our intimacy with Him. His promise to the resolute heart is a deep, fulfilling "dining" (or communion) with Him – leading to the fulfillment of His purposes. When it is all said and done, that is all that matters.

Lord, teach us (and motivate us) to pray.

Idle Prayer Words

"But I say to you that for every idle wordmen may speak, they will give account of it in the day of judgement."

Matthew 12:36

One of my least favorite verses in the Bible states that God will hold us accountable for every "idle word" we speak. I have systematically avoided preaching on this passage over the years, probably because it is too convicting. But in recent weeks, the Lord has deeply challenged my heart about the subject of idle words, especially as it relates to our teaching and practices in prayer.

The context for Matthew 12:33-37 can be summed up in one word: "Pharisees." In vv. 1 & 2 they were denouncing Christ because He and His disciples were violating their laws. In v.13 they were trying to destroy Him because He posed a threat to their religious systems. In v. 24 they were demonizing Jesus. In v. 38 they were trying to distract Him with a demand for signs. Jesus was in the midst of another series of confrontations with established religious leaders who spoke many of the right things but whose hearts were clearly not in the right place.

Matthew 12:33-37 records Jesus' response to them. He notes that their words were good – but their hearts were not right. He noted, "Out of the abundance of the heart the mouth speaks" (v. 34). Then he said,

"But I say to you that for every idle word men may speak, they will give account of it in the day of judgment. For by your words you will be justified, and by your words you will be condemned" (vv. 36-37).

Words that Don't Work

What are idle words? We know that words are powerful. The Bible says that death and life are in the power of the tongue. We are cautioned against deceptive, malicious, unwholesome, lying, and false words. But what are these idle words of which religious people can become so guilty?

In the Greek, the word translated "idle" is "argon," which literally means, "not working." Idle words are inoperative, inactive words. In historical writing this word was used to describe words that are lazy and void of the labor they ought to perform. These are words that are unprofitable even though they should be productive. It is the same word used in James 2:20 where it says, "But do you want to know, O foolish man, that faith without works is dead?" The idea of something "without works" is the same as the concept of "idle" words.

Why should we have a particular concern about idle words? For those of us in the American Church, we must tune in to this passage because we are blessed with such an abundance of words. We have religious words flowing in unprecedented fashion via radio, television, books, magazines, and downloads, in addition to our daily conversations. Yet we know that those who call themselves Christ-followers in our society do not live much differently than unbelievers. In this case, our words are idle words because they are empty and unprofitable and do not result in the intended works.

Matthew 15:8 presents Jesus quoting the words of God from the book of Isaiah: "These people draw near to Me with their mouth, and honor Me with their lips, but their heart is far from Me." Some believe that we are the most over-informed but under-exercised generation in the history of Christianity. This is the mark of many idle words.

A Common Concern

Why are idle prayer words so common? I have a special concern about idle words in the arena of prayer. I have been speaking at a national prayer conference, and I have been astounded with all the prayer materials that are available and all the books that are being written on prayer. I have personally written books on prayer and speak on prayer often. I heard a leader note that more books have been written on prayer in the last 30 years than in the previous 300 years combined. To whom much is given, much is required. If the words do not result in the actual work of prayer, they are idle words.

It is easy to speak and write on prayer because we all know in our soul that prayer words are right words, biblical words, and God-honoring words. We know that prayer is essential in our lives, our churches, and our nation. But often, talking about prayer is much easier than spending time in actual prayer.

This is the case for many because our experiences of prayer are not positive. I heard a leader say, "The reason many Christians do not attend prayer meetings is because they attended prayer meetings." Too often what passes in the name of prayer is dull, unbiblical, laborious, and counterproductive.

Prayer is at the focal point of spiritual warfare, so the enemy does all he can to keep us from the work of prayer. Of course, real prayer requires the investment of our most precious commodity – time. Some struggle with prayer because they are angry at God or fear real intimacy with Him. Yet all the while, we can talk about prayer with relative ease.

A Practical Danger

What is the danger of idle prayer words? Idle prayer words are dangerous because we can become inoculated against actually carrying out our words. James 1:22-25 says, "But be doers of the word, and not hearers only, deceiving yourselves. For if anyone is a hearer of the word and not a doer, he is like a man observing his natural face in a mirror; for he observes himself, goes away, and immediately forgets what kind of man he was." Truth unapplied results in self-deception and blinds us from the real blessings of the power of biblical application. We think we are okay because we have heard words, even though we are not putting them into practice.

Jesus' words in Matthew 12 implicate us: "But I say to you that for every idle word men may speak, they will give account of it in the day of judgment." Clearly, idle words are a great concern to Christ – and they should be to us, too.

It is good to remember that Jesus did not say that His house would be a house of information about prayer. In 1 Timothy 2:1 Paul did not say that "first of all" we are to preach about prayer. In Acts 6:4 the early church leaders did not give themselves continually to discussions about prayer. No, the only real option in honoring God's word is to actually pray.

How do we engage in idle prayer words? There are many ways in which we engage in idle prayer words. At a personal level it occurs when we read books about prayer and talk about prayer, but do not pray commensurately with our information flow. In families, idle prayer words occur when we give lip service to prayer but fail to pray with our spouses, children, and family members. In ministries, idle prayer words flow when we talk about the need to pray about things – but don't set aside time and actually pray.

Idle prayer words are probably most common in the pulpits of our land. Sermons on prayer are abundant. Churches that pray are not.

In his classic book *Lectures to My Students*, Charles Spurgeon addresses our tendency towards idle words when he writes,

> *"The minister who does not earnestly pray over his work must surely be a vain and conceited man. He acts as if he thought himself sufficient of himself, and therefore needed not to appeal to God... The preacher*

who neglects to pray much must be very careless about his ministry. He cannot have comprehended his calling. He cannot have computed the value of a soul or estimated the meaning of eternity. He must be a mere official, tempted into a pulpit because the piece of bread which belongs to the priest's office is very necessary to him, or a detestable hypocrite who loves the praise of men, and cares not for the praise of God. He will surely become a mere superficial talker, best approved where grace is least valued and a vain show most admired. He cannot be one of those who plows deep and reaps abundant harvests. He is a mere loiterer, not a laborer. As a preacher he has a name to live and is dead. He limps in his life like the lame man in Proverbs, whose legs were not equal, for his praying is shorter than his preaching.[23]

Strong words indeed. Yet they serve as a great reminder that a pastor's sermons on prayer that are not followed by a commitment to pray, and do not lead one's people in prayer, are but empty words.

I have a good pastor friend who preached on prayer every Sunday for a year but later confessed that it did not make a difference in the prayer level of his people. He realized that it is better to lead people in prayer than to preach at people about prayer. First Corinthians 4:20 says, "For the kingdom of God is not in word but in power."

(Part Two)

Idle Prayer Words

"For by your words you will be justified, and by your words wou will be condemned."

Matthew 12:37

How easy it is to fall into the trap of empty words and say much about prayer but end up giving most of our attention to more words, music, entertainment, and fellowship, with no designated time to really engage in substantive prayer.

What should we do about it? If we find our hearts convicted about idle words, what can we do? Here are a few brief points of encouragement.

Seek Restoration

As Jesus said in the context of Matthew 12, either make the tree good and its fruit good, or else make the tree bad and its fruit bad; for a tree is known by its fruit. This is a call to ask God to restore a true and good heart that desires God, seeks Him, and spends time with Him in a desire for relationship over rhetoric.

Seek Recalibration

Sometimes we need to do something radical to recalibrate our souls. A three–day retreat in solitude and prayer can rekindle our love for His presence. A time of fasting might break the stronghold of contentment with empty words.

Seek Application

With every book on prayer you read and every discussion on prayer you have, seek to apply the truths immediately by praying in the moment or in the hours to follow. Learn the grace of putting prayer truths into action with intentional determination. As J. Oswald Sanders reminds us, "The only way to learn to pray is by praying, and the real estimate of the place of prayer will be seen in the amount of time we give to it."[24] Or, as the Nike Company says, "Just Do It." I have over-analyzed, organized, theorized, strategized – and now I need but to lift my eyes to the one who sees, knows, and brings truth into my life – and graciously wants to draw me to Himself in fact – not just in word.

Seek Initiation

If words far outweigh our prayers, it would be good to initiate some fresh times of prayer that will allow a fresh and consistent experience of fellowship with Jesus.

Seek Coalition

Ask a friend or associate to pray with you on a consistent basis. Not only will you enjoy the encouragement of their fellowship, but you will find joy in allocating more time to grow in the privilege of prayer.

My Personal Struggle

As a pastor over the years, I have tried to challenge my heart toward less talk and more prayer. I remember arriving at Arcade Church in 1993 with a desire for renewal. I had the burden to draw the church into prayer by the experience of doing it – more than talking about it. God allowed us to have our first three-day Prayer Summit, which was a profound lesson in the experience of prayer. In the years to follow, I did not preach on prayer very often. I did not need to. The people of Arcade just kept praying via several summits per year and multiple weekly prayer meetings. God delivered us from idle words and just helped us to pray.

However, when I went from being a senior pastor to becoming a "spiritual pyromaniac" for the cause of renewal, the challenge became much more serious. Now I travel 35-40 times a year talking about prayer. I speak on prayer at Liberty University and teach on prayer at my local church. I am regularly writing on prayer in books and magazines. The drift into more information and less intimacy is very real to me and a great concern to my heart.

Not Guilt but Glory!

The point of all of this is not to impose guilt, but to inspire glory. Second Corinthians 3:18-4:1 says, "But we all, with unveiled face, beholding as in a mirror the glory of the Lord, are being transformed into the same image from glory to glory, just as by the Spirit of the Lord. Therefore, since we have this ministry, as we have received mercy, we do not lose heart...."

The world will not be changed by the overabundance of our information, but by the overflow of our intimacy. So the cry of my heart in these days is, "Less talk – more prayer!" Where there is less talk and more prayer there will be more joy and less worry. We will have more of His presence and less of our presentations. There will be more unity and less division – more supernatural power and less superficial striving. We will experience more divine miracles with less human manipulation and more passion for the lost with less programming for the saved.

This is the blessing of aligning our hearts and our words toward an authentic pursuit of God through prayer. We will experience His glory here on earth and give Him greater glory someday in heaven.

Pastors Coming Out of the Closet

"But we will give ourselves continually to ptrayer and to the ministry of the word."

Acts 6:4

Recently I conducted a Renewal Weekend at a large mid-western church. The pastor is an educated, articulate leader known for his preaching acumen. He even writes books to help preachers create effective sermons.

After the final service of the weekend (a Sunday evening worship-based prayer experience) he stood before his church with tears and offered two observations. First, he stated that he had not experienced the presence of God in such a powerful way since his early days in ministry where revival broke out in the church where he served on staff. Indeed, it was a powerful evening of worship and heart-felt prayer.

His second observation was incredibly insightful. He said to his congregation, "Over the years I've told you that the corporate prayer level of our church will never rise above our personal prayer lives." He continued, "Tonight I want to correct that statement. I have concluded that our personal prayer lives will never rise above our corporate prayer experience because this is how we all learn to pray – in community. And I am resolved to lead you in that experience that we might truly become a house of prayer."

You could conclude that this courageous pastor decided to come out of his prayer closet and start leading his people in the actual experience of prayer. That decision has been a big victory for him, for his congregation, and for Christ-honoring ministry in that community.

Toward a Consistent View of Leadership
Of course, it is an essential and wonderful thing that many pastors prioritize personal time in prayer. However, far too few come to the conviction of this pastor in the firm understanding that they must lead their people in prayer by example while modeling prayer in community experience. In reality, they are adopting a view of leadership that leaves their people far short of Christ's ideal for the church.

Let me illustrate. Imagine a pastor named Charlie. He claims to have a deep conviction about the importance of the Bible in his life and ministry. He speaks highly of the Scriptures in personal conversations and writes compellingly about it in his philosophy of ministry. He claims to have a strong personal regimen of Bible reading and study. Yet, the pattern of this leadership demonstrates an actual contradiction. In his public ministry Charlie is apathetic about the existence of Bible studies in his church. He never teaches people how to study the Bible. He seldom leads any Bible studies with others. When he does on those rare occasions, he seems uncomfortable and half-hearted. In spite of Charlie's verbal assent about the benefit of the Bible, he makes minimal references to the Scriptures when the church gathers. He rarely invests any substantive amount of time teaching the Bible to his congregation in corporate worship on Sundays. Instead, he tells stories and packs the services with an abundance of music, drama, and interesting anecdotes about current events.

Any church worth their salt would be grieved about the contradiction of Pastor Charlie's words. They would wonder about his real commitment to the centrality of the Scriptures. While Charlie might talk a good talk, he obviously is failing to lead his church in the love for and understanding of the Bible.

In fact, the real commodity by which we judge any pastor's commitment to the Scriptures is *time*. This includes time spent personally in the Word but ALSO time given to teaching and experiencing the power of applied truth in the corporate gatherings. If he does not give time to the Bible, we rightfully conclude he does not really value it.

Leading from the Closet Does Not Work

When it comes to prayer, many pastors live in the same contradictory gray twilight as Charlie. Somehow flowery words about prayer and claims of "doing business with God" in "the closet" suffice, while the church starves for leadership, never really learning how to pray. Jesus grieves because His house does not become a house of prayer. The Apostle Paul's words in 1 Timothy 2 indicating that the church should *first* be a place of prayer are essentially ignored – because no one is leading the church in that direction. The commands to pray, given in the New Testament, are largely ignored in the community experience of the church.

In my travels, I see this so often. Many respected and godly leaders purport to have a strong prayer life – in private. However, they appear to have little conviction about modeling prayer and leading their people into life-changing experiences of prayer (we will talk about the reasons later). Of course, these pastors never lead powerful, praying churches because it is impossible to *point* the way in prayer. One must *lead* the way in prayer.

Just as you cannot lead the church in the ministry of the word simply from a desk, neither can you lead a church in prayer simply from a closet. In Acts 6:4 the early leaders were committed to engaging collectively and leading the church in BOTH prayer and the ministry of the word. Today, like those leaders, pastors must come out of their private closets and provide bold, biblical, and consistent leadership.

Why Church Leaders Hide in t b bheir Prayer Closets

Let me say clearly that the value of private prayer is beyond measure. Responsible pastors seek the Lord individually and regularly intercede for others. Yet, too many good pastors seem content with leaving their prayer impact at the closet door. Why is this?

In my book *Fresh Encounters*, I wrote extensively about this challenge – based on my own struggle in prayer and conversations with many pastoral colleagues. In summary, our reluctance to lead our churches in prayer is rooted in the following factors:

1. Rugged individualism
2. Closet confusion
3. Limited vision
4. Inadequate training
5. Cultural pushback
6. Personal defeat
7. Spiritual distraction
8. Fear of intimacy

In the next chapter, we will elaborate on each of these eight factors and encourage your heart with some truths about the blessings that occur when pastors come out of their prayer closets to lead their people in biblical, balanced prayer.

In the meantime, pray for your pastor today. Pray that the Lord will draw him close to His heart and teach him more about the joys of seeking God's face. Pray that, in His time, the Lord will help him see the calling to lead the church in regular and life-giving experiences of prayer. In the meantime, keep a loving and supportive attitude and look for opportunities to make a difference on your knees in your own church. The Lord will bless you as you support your leadership and pray for their growth in Christ.

(Part Two)

Pastors Coming Out of the Closet

"But we will give ourselves continually to ptrayer and to the ministry of the word."

Acts 6:4

We have observed that many pastors in the church today are reluctant to give consistent, bold, and enduring public leadership to prayer in their churches. We concluded that just as a pastor cannot lead the church in the ministry of the word simply from a desk, neither can you lead a church in prayer simply from a "closet." The kind of leadership that creates a culture of prayer in a church requires pastoral modeling and participation in a community context.

Of course, private prayer is essential. The Scripture calls spiritual leaders to seek the Lord individually and regularly intercede for others. Yet, too many good pastors seem content with leaving their prayer impact at the closet door. Why is this?

Why Church Leaders Remain in Their Prayer Closets

In my book Fresh Encounters, I wrote extensively about these issues based on my own struggle in prayer and conversations with many pastoral colleagues. As I see it, our reluctance to lead our churches in prayer is rooted in the eight following factors:

Rugged individualism – Perhaps the defining characteristic of Western Civilization is rugged individualism. Professor and Pastor Gene Getz notes that our "lens" of individualism causes us to re-interpret the prayer commands in the New Testament, making them individual in application when they were really given in a community context in the early churches, and applied accordingly. Today, we can easily conclude that it is sufficient simply to pray in an individual setting.

Closet Confusion – We have misunderstood the meaning of the place of prayer in Matthew 6 where Jesus is giving group instructions to His disciples about their prayer lives. Even though the model prayer is composed entirely of plural pronouns ("Our Father...give us..."), we have turned their upper room into a solitary cubicle based on our own cultural overlay and unfortunate misunderstanding of the word "closet" (used only in the 1611 KJV). Again, I have two chapters about this in *Fresh Encounters.*

Limited Vision – Most pastors have never really experienced a positive example of a dynamic, praying church. What many of us did experience was counterproductive in the form of request-based gatherings that include endless lists of physical needs, some discussion, and even a little gossip – but little real prayer. I often note the Brazilian proverb that says, "The heart cannot taste what the eyes have not seen." Without the living vision and experience of transforming prayer, it is hard to understand the clear path to bold, enduring leadership.

Inadequate Training – Bible colleges and seminaries marginalize prayer when training pastors. Seldom is there even one entire class devoted to the subject of prayer. Many seminary leaders omit prayer because it is not "academic" enough. They subvert the biblical requirements for pastoral leadership in the name of scholarship. Virtually every pastor I know admits that college and seminary offered very little training in how to develop a prayer culture or lead a church in prayer as a pastor. We just assume they will "get it." Most often, they do not.

Cultural Pushback – Our quick fix, results-oriented culture expects a pastor to be a program-producing CEO who speaks, manages, and runs to the next meeting with Wall-Street pizzazz. These expectations can leave a pastor with little margin and waning motivation for real impact in prayer.

Personal Defeat – Some pastors are defeated in their own prayer life and do not feel adequate to lead in prayer. Yet, if they start leading, everyone prays more – including the pastor. Prayer grows and deepens. The ministry wins.

Spiritual distraction – The devil does not have to destroy a pastor; he simply needs to distract a pastor. The devil is not too troubled by talent, education, charisma, and administrative ability. A praying pastor who has taken up the powerful weapons of spiritual warfare to fight the good fight – by praying always, personally and in community, threatens the enemy.

Fear of intimacy – Because so many of us have grown up with such relational dysfunction, we carry a low-grade fear of real, wholesome intimacy. This is evident in marriages, in friendships, and in the church. We see it among pastors as well. Because prayer is an exercise of spiritual intimacy, praying in community is often avoided.

The Blessing of Coming Out of the Closet

One of the great joys of my life is the experience of watching churches grow into a life-giving congregation that exhibits a real culture of prayer. Not only have I known the grace and joy of seeing this happen in the congregations I have served – but also every year I am with pastors around the nation who are providing essential public prayer leadership for their people. The blessings abound when this occurs:

Christ-honoring Ministry – The Lord is delighted when a church truly becomes a "house of prayer" (Mark 11:17) and when they implement Paul's command that the church pray "first of all" (1 Timothy 2:1). Christ is exalted when the kingdom advancements in a ministry are directly attributed to the Spirit of God in connection with the prayer activity of the church. This correlation points to the power of God rather than the wisdom of men (1 Corinthians 2:5).

Spiritual Health – Congregational health emerges when a Spirit-energized movement of prayer grows in a congregation. Believers who experience the power of worship-based prayer enjoy a genuine unity of heart and mind. Trust is strengthened as hearts connect in worship and believing prayer.

Missional Impact – Just as the early church could not help but speak of what they had seen and heard (Acts 4:20), praying churches are empowered and equipped to share the gospel, reach out to the needy, plant churches, and expand their global outreach. The Holy Spirit is a witness-bearing Spirit and real prayer brings Christians more fully under practical surrender to the Spirit's control.

Manifest Presence – Praying churches experience the reality of 2 Corinthians 3:18 as they collectively behold the glory of the Lord and are transformed from "glory to glory" into Christ's image by the power of the Spirit. It is common for church guests to be gripped by a sense of the presence of God. Every pastor longs for his church to be identified by the reality of the manifest presence of Christ. Praying churches tend to enjoy an authentic experience of this reality.

Following the Spirit's Direction into New Experiences of His Blessings

In truth, many other benefits and blessings accompany a growing, pastor-led prayer culture. Let us make it our collective prayer that these positive realities will become the norm in our nation.

Today, if you are a pastor, I pray that you will ultimately sense the Spirit's clear direction for your life and ministry as He guides you into a growing realm of influence in prayer in your church. He is always faithful to direct and to provide the time and energy for the things that are close to the heart of Christ.

If you are a church member, continue to pray for a greater movement of God's Spirit in awakening the church and her leaders to their need to seek God's face. Keep a godly and supportive heart as you find opportunities to engage in prayer with others in your church. If the Lord wants this kind of movement to occur (and we believe that He does), He will continue to prompt hearts and orchestrate opportunities.

Stay Weak!

"For our gospel did not come to you in word only, but also in power, and in the Holy Spirit and in much assurance, as you know what kind of men we were among you for your sake."

1 Thessalonians 1:5

Paul's description and approach seem like such a contrast to what we often see in the pulpits of our nation. His emphasis throughout his Scriptural letters is never on human savvy, but always on the supernatural power of the Holy Spirit. He had full assurance in the sufficiency of the Scripture and Spirit – and, as he says, he sought to be an example of this power in the way he lived.

Avoiding the Extremes

In our humanity it seems that we tend toward two extremes in comparison to Paul's ideal. Often we attempt to be clever through our human ingenuity and love affair with the intellectual. Our technological advancement perpetuates this tendency. We live in an age of impressive preachers and clever sermons.

The other extreme is what I call "concocted" spiritual power. We work hard to create the atmosphere (a pathetic blend of emotion and hype) then label it Holy Spirit power. It's problematically based on the amount of excessive behavior we can work up in the service. Both extremes seem manufactured to me.

The secret to real power in the pulpit is no secret at all. It is recognized, genuinely-embraced weakness. Hear Paul's words in a different context: "And I, brethren, when I came to you, did not come with excellence of speech or of wisdom declaring to you the testimony of God. For I determined not to know anything among you except Jesus Christ and Him crucified. I was with you in weakness, in fear, and in much trembling. And my speech and my preaching were not with persuasive words of human wisdom, but in demonstration of the Spirit and of power, that your faith should not be in the wisdom of men but in the power of God" (1 Corinthians 2:1-5).

The Lord Jesus told Paul in no uncertain terms that His strength was made perfect in Paul's weakness (2 Corinthians 12:9). Our problem with this truth is that weakness is not an attractive thing to us. It is counter-intuitive and counter-cultural. But it is imperative to a ministry fueled by the Holy Spirit.

We must be like Paul in cultivating a holy fear and a trembling heart in view of the high calling God has placed on our lives. We must embrace the impossibility of accomplishing supernatural works in the power of our human excellence, earthly wisdom, and persuasive speech. Our talent, intellect, preparation, and planning can be useful tools, but they are a miserable and dangerous source.

The Fruit of Weakness

So what does this mean? I think that every spiritual leader and every believer must seek to function with this mindset everyday. We do this by staying focused on the sufficiency of Christ and His cross, and making it the passion and message of our lives. We do this by living in awe of His power and staying ever cautious of our own flesh. We must choose weakness as a fruit of this worship.

Prayer is the practical demonstration of our humility and dependence on God. Prayerlessness is our declaration of independence from God. So, we must bathe and support everything we do in sincere and humble prayer. It is a paradox.

I love the way a Puritan writer describes it in the book, Valley of Vision:

> *Let me learn by paradox*
> *That the way down is the way up,*
> *That to be low is to be high,*
> *That the broken heart is the healed heart,*
> *That the contrite spirit if the rejoicing spirit,*
> *That the repenting soul is the victorious soul,*
> *That to have nothing is to possess all,*
> *That to bear the cross is to wear the crown,*
> *That to give is to receive,*
> *That the valley is the place of vision.*[25]

As you go to the office today, as you interact with neighbors, as you care for your children, as you enjoy your vacation, as you lead a ministry, here's the best advice: stay weak. Let His power have authority in your thoughts, words and deeds. We will turn the eyes of a watching world toward the supremacy and sufficiency of Jesus Christ.

A Cultivated Desperation
"...have no confidence in the flesh."

Pjilippians 3:3

Christ responds in extraordinary fashion to desperate, hungry, and passionate souls. Conversely, He is saddened by self-sufficient, luke-warm hearts. So, do we feel desperate today? If not, can we?

I preach often about the fact that we can get desperate either through crisis or cultivation. God is in charge of the crisis. It is always interesting to analyze the "signs of the times," economic indicators, and political developments to assess how this might be unfolding. But ultimately, God can step in at any moment to create desperation in the hearts of His people through extraordinary and difficult circumstances.

But, I also believe Christ calls us to cultivate desperation. In a sense, this is the passion of Strategic Renewal – to help cultivate a heart of spiritual desperation in the American church. The Bible is full of urgings to repent, acknowledge needs, seek His face, and endure to the end. One of the best New Testament pictures of desperation is seen in Philippians 3.

The Commitments of a Desperate Man

This chapter is marked by emotionally-packed words describing Paul's cultivated desperation. Expressions like "press on," "lay hold," "apprehend," "reaching forward," "press toward the goal," and "the upward call" highlight this potent description of Paul's spiritual quest. This is a great snapshot of the vocabulary and vision of a desperate heart. So, what can we learn from Paul if we are to experience the blessing of spiritual desperation? How can we cultivate this necessary attitude on a daily basis? Two components of Paul's commitment are found in the daily calculations he made and the core understanding he embraced.

The Calculations of a Desperate Man

Using familiar accounting terms, Paul describes the regular "P & L" system of his heart. The profit and loss columns were very clear in his mind. I believe it would be safe to label the profit column with the word "delight." Over the loss column, you could place the word "dung." On a constant basis Paul populated the "dung" column with ideas like "religious works," "self-reliant righteousness," and any human-originated systems of "goodness" that competed with the sufficiency of the person and work of Christ.

In the often-quoted epicenter of this passage, Paul declares his resolve to pursue and profit from the "excellence of the knowledge of Christ Jesus." He speaks openly of his longing to "gain Christ and be found in Him." He declares his determination to "know Christ" and "the power of His resurrection, the fellowship of His sufferings, being conformed to His death, if, by any means (he) might attain to the resurrection from the dead."

These words, from Philippians 3:7-11, are the expressions of a spiritually desperate and determined heart with a clearly defined "profit" column. This regular discipline of spiritual accounting kept Paul desperate, focused, and useful in the Master's hand.

The Core of a Desperate Man

Using some of his most colorful language, Paul begins this chapter by contrasting the core of spiritual desperation with the dangerous complacency of religious self-reliance. He writes, "Beware of dogs, beware of evil workers, beware of the mutilation! For we are the circumcision, who worship God in the Spirit, rejoice in Christ Jesus, and have no confidence in the flesh" (Philippians 3:2-3).

Circumcision was not a bad thing in the Scriptures. It was an outward, distinctive trait of God's covenant people, the Jews. But the great enemies of a Christ-centered spiritual desperation are the common and acceptable elements of respectable religion.

Referring to those who traded spiritual passion for religious observances as the essence of their faith, Paul called them dogs, evil workers, and mutilators. That is strong language. Dogs were scavengers, menaces and symbols of uncleanness.

Religious devotion is seldom viewed as "evil," but Paul describes it this way because anything that displaces a passion for the centrality of Christ is a great evil to the soul. Mutilation seems extreme to describe circumcision – but if it takes away from a passion for Jesus, it amounts to meaningless bodily torture.

(Part Two)
A Cultivated
Desperation
"...have no confidence in the flesh."

Pjilippians 3:3

The great threat to the integrity of our monetary system is not Monopoly money but counterfeit bills. The lurking danger to a marriage is not the beautiful actress in the magazine but the overly friendly co-worker at the office. Spiritual revival is not threatened by radical Islam but by the easy alternatives of religious systems that we substitute for a passion for Christ. Paul's point is that religious observances that displace a Christ-centered spiritual desperation (especially when they are imposed upon us in a legalistic spirit) are menaces and, ultimately, evil replacements.

Today, the threat of "circumcision" could be identified with church attendance, philanthropic works, standards of "Christian behavior," and a whole list of specific rules that are imposed in a legalistic way as marks of spirituality. They seem good – but are ultimately dangerous and evil if elevated above a pure passion for Christ. They can become extinguishers of our desperation because they give us a false sense of spiritual devotion.

So here now is the core of Paul's heart of spiritual desperation. He calls it the real "circumcision" because it defines a devoted heart, not just an adapted anatomy. He lists three things that drive him away from the superficial replacements and propel him deeper into a genuine and burning spiritual pursuit.

Worship God in the Spirit – Paul echoes the heart of Jesus' words from John 4:24, "God is Spirit, and those who worship Him must worship in spirit and truth." We know that real worship is not a matter of rules and religious forms – but we can easily drift into a drowsy routine of going through the motions. Paul puts forth the priority of Spirit-guided, Spirit-empowered, Spirit-sensitive worship – not just on Sundays, but every day.

Rejoice in Christ Jesus – Paul is declaring here that all his joy, his focus, his bragging, and his glory are in Jesus and Jesus alone. As author David Bryant declares, "Christ is all."

Have no confidence in the flesh – Here is a complete turning away from any Christ-replacements. All human efforts, religious duties, or man-made systems that would in any way justify ourselves or elevate our works are flatly rejected. This daily, perhaps minute-by-minute, vote of no confidence helped Paul keep a desperate heart.

So, having considered all of this – what are our applications for this day?

• First, we must keep our sights high. We must speak an think regularly of pressing onward and upward, becoming engaged in the call and finishing our race with passion.

• We must conduct a daily accounting with correct entries in the "dung" and "delight" columns.

• We must stay free of the trap of legalistic, heartless religion and pursue a consistent, Spirit-empowered life of genuine worship.

• We must focus our hearts on Christ alone so that the love and language of all we do is about Him.

• We must recognize the ever-present reality of "the flesh" and cast an instinctive, decisive vote of no confidence every time it raises its ugly head to take credit for anything good in our lives.

Perhaps these things will help us journey toward a cultivated desperation for Christ. In that position we will find blessing, power, joy, and supernatural impact on our culture. Anything less will miss the mark.

Beholding, Becoming, Behaving

"Therefore, since we have this ministry, as we have received mercy, we do not lose heart."

2 Corinthians 4:1

During one of the most difficult seasons of my pastoral ministry, the Lord graciously led me in a verse-by-verse study of the book of 2 Corinthians. The power and practicality of this book kept my mind and heart rooted in truth, at a time in which I desperately needed it.

As you may know, 2 Corinthians is one of Paul's most transparent epistles. He wrote to a troubled congregation in whom he had previously invested eighteen months of his life. Sadly, they had been infiltrated by false teachers that were launching an all-out assault on Paul's ministry and character. Paul wrote the letter to defend his apostleship and communicate the heart of credible ministry. As he wrote, he opened his heart wide.

I've come to believe that 2 Corinthians 2:14 -7:1 are the core verses describing outstanding Christian leadership. And at the core of these verses is 2 Corinthians 3:18-4:7. As I reflect on these essential truths, three words clearly emerge: beholding, becoming and behaving.

Pursuing the Relationship

At the center of all authentic Christian faith and growth, we find the truth of 2 Corinthians 3:18: "But we all, with unveiled face, beholding as in a mirror the glory of the Lord, are being transformed into the same image from glory to glory, just as by the Spirit of the Lord."

Because of the New Covenant secured by the death, burial and resurrection of Christ, every believer now has the privilege of full and free access to the person and presence of God (3:17). What was once limited only to Moses or the Old Testament high priests is now our great privilege. We are beholding the glory of the Lord as we gaze upon Christ through eyes of faith, by the power of the Holy Spirit and the means of God's Word and prayer. This represents our pursuit of an intimate relationship with Christ.

Real beholding results in becoming. We are "transformed into the same image," the image and character of Christ. This growing transformation is an ever-increasing change at the core of who we are. This happens from "glory to glory," or greater degrees of Christ-likeness day-by-day.

As a result of beholding and becoming, our behavior is affected. Here is the great truth that we must continually embrace: behaving is the fruit of becoming, and becoming is the result of beholding. If all we do is focus on our behavior, we will have a shallow lifestyle that conforms on the outside, but it does not experience transformation on the inside. When we enjoy an intimate "beholding," we will be Christ-like in our becoming, and ultimately Christ-honoring in our behaving.

The Best Focus

Unfortunately, too often we simply behave dutifully, striving to obey while neglecting our time with the Lord. Like Martha, we are eager to please and motivated to serve. If our activity does not reflect Christ-like character, we will fall short of the goal of eternally significant impact.

Conversely, when we keep the discipline and privilege of beholding at the epicenter of our lives, we will become more like Christ. Our ministry will be the overflow of this spiritual reality. Like Mary, who sat at Jesus' feet and listened to His word in focused communion, we will receive the commendation of choosing the "best part" that will not be taken away (Luke 10:42).

I recently heard someone say, "Our great fear is not that we will fail, but that we will succeed in things that do not really matter." Let me encourage you to behold His glory today as you seek His face and feed on His Word. You will be conformed to His image, and your service will be sincere and supernatural. And someday, you will be facing the Lord, presenting a life of gold, silver and precious stones, rather than the wood, hay and stubble of a dutiful but distracted life.

Organic vs. Organizational Revival

"Your kingdom come..."

Matthew 6:10

These days it seems every Christian is trying to drum up excitement for another revival event. There is no shortage of ideas afloat about how we all need to converge at some big gathering to instill a transforming touch among the masses of eager hearts that travel far and wide to find a new angle on prayer and renewal.

Some of these gatherings are designed to call down God's fire, while others focus on the need to wait quietly on the Lord's "word." I am sure the organizers are sincere and dedicated. Each has some biblical guidelines that motivate all the activity.

Yet all of these gatherings are very expensive and complicated to organize. The promotional machinery involved in making these events occur is nothing less than gargantuan. The dollars flow like water as the lights, cameras, and action are all prepared for the big day when God will show up. In some cases, celebrity Christians are the key to attracting a crowd. In most cases, I suppose many walk away wondering who really got the credit for the big event – and who kept the leftover cash.

I am among those who have a burning desire for revival and a passionate commitment to prayer – but with all the hype, I am feeling a bit "hustled" these days. It seems we are all expected to deliver on some imaginative dream that may or may not be of God. It feels like we are expected to finance someone else's visionary grandiosity. Honestly, I find myself wondering if this is really the Lord's best plan for reviving His church.

An Alternative Approach

I am dreaming of something more organic; something arising as a natural outgrowth.

In the rush of getting God to show up at another revival event, I wonder if we really need to slow down, tone down, and get down to the humble, quiet, grassroots spiritual labor that typifies revivals. At least, these seem to be the ingredients of revivals that last more than a day or two.

In my ministry, I am coming to realize that God has graciously given us a vision that is basically organic. It is focused on revival arising as a natural outgrowth of desire for Christ. Our ministry's vision statement reads: "Pastor-led, local church-oriented movements of Christ-exalting, worship-based prayer – leading to a full-scale revival, supernatural evangelism and cultural transformation."

Essentially, it is our desire to equip pastors and churches to become houses of prayer with spiritual passion and endurance. The goal is clearly not the elevation of any church, ministry or personality – but that Christ would receive glory as congregations around the nation awaken to His purposes and presence. The prayer movement that we envision is worship-based – not request-, confession- or warfare-based. The latter all flow out of the former. Worship-based prayer cultivates a passion for His honor and a deep repentance in His presence.

We believe that as pastors and churches grow in an extraordinary commitment to His word and prayer, a full-scale revival could occur as the water level of genuine renewal rises across the country in congregations from the North, South, East and West – large and small, and of various denominational stripes. Out of this revival, we envision profound evangelism occurring, as it historically occurred in previous revivals. Ultimately, we believe the culture will be transformed by the gospel as demonstrated through the glorious church in the New Testament. Then the tide will turn.

Evaluating the Options

In closing, perhaps it helps to contrast these two approaches to revival:

• Organizational revival can be personality-driven. Organic revival is process-focused.

• Organizational revival costs a lot of money. Organic revival demands a lot of time, overtime, on our knees.

• Organizational revival is driven by events. Organic revival is focused on equipping.

• Organizational revival depends on slick promotion. Organic revival thrives on sacrificial prayer.

• Organizational revival sometimes features hyped-up spiritual cheerleaders. Organic revival is sparked by humble, praying pastors and saints in quiet places across the land.

• Organizational revival potentially convolutes the focus on Christ's supreme glory. Organic revival longs for a nondescript, broad, and unpredictable movement that exalts only His name.

• Organizational revival can be driven by the activities on the stage in a big arena. Organic revival is nurtured by intercessors on their faces in local church gatherings.

Ultimately, organic revival must start with my heart, my home, my church and my community. If you pray that for me – and I pray that for you – and if we act in faith to seek His face, something organic and glorious might just occur. It is worth dreaming about, worth seeking after and worth living for. Thanks for joining me in this quest for the glory of Christ.

Seasonal Thoughts

"You only go around once in life;
grab all of the reality you can."

Strange Way to Say Happy Birthday

"For unto us a Child is born, Unto us a Son is given."

Isaiah 9:6

Imagine a large home filled with people who have come to celebrate the birthday of a beloved friend. Let's call him Jessie. Scores of acquaintances, work associates, neighbors and family members gather together. The volume is deafening as individuals reconnect, recollect and enjoy the excitement of the occasion.

Somehow, as the night unfolds everyone becomes so engaged in the activity that they forget all about Jessie. There is no song, no cake, no card or gifts for him to open. But everyone still has a jovial time. Then another oddity occurs. People actually bring presents to the party, but they are designated for others in attendance. The gifts are opened cheerfully. Each one reflects the great care, thoughtfulness and sacrifice of the giver, and each recipient thoroughly appreciates the gift he receives.

Very briefly, a few people do finally pause to remember Jessie, after the crowd has dissipated. But it feels almost like an afterthought. They remember to grab some gifts from the car – but Jessie has the distinct feeling that the presents are impersonal and spur-of-the-moment. After all is said and done, Jessie did not even receive anything he wanted for his birthday.

As the last guest leaves, Jessie turns to his wife with a look of obvious disillusionment. His wife tries to comfort him by saying, "Sorry Jessie, we all just got carried away. I guess we kind of forgot why we all got together." Jessie wanders off to bed dejected, almost wishing this day had never happened. It all seemed like a very strange way to say "Happy Birthday."

The Right Way to Celebrate

Does this sound curiously familiar? It may reflect the reality of how we say "Happy Birthday" to Jesus all too often. Let's consider some alternative and more appropriate ideas about how to observe the birth of our Lord as we look at a group of Christ-honoring celebrants who got it right.

If I were forced to choose, I would probably select the Magi as my favorite characters in the Christmas story (other than baby Jesus, of course). In a sense, they are the antithesis to our opening story about Jessie and his birthday guests.

These mysterious sages understood a reality that entire societies of the day missed. It was someone's birthday. The wise men knew it was someone special, as evidenced in their words, "Where is He who has been born King of the Jews? For we have seen His star in the East and have come to worship Him." (Matthew 2:2). They later quoted their study of the Old Testament prophet Micah when they described this newborn as *a Ruler who will shepherd My people Israel.* That passage in Micah further states that this Ruler would be one "whose goings forth are from of old, from everlasting." The Magi knew this was no ordinary child.

When the Magi's journey ended, they found the "child" in a house (which may indicate they arrived months after his birth, perhaps up to two years into Christ's life). In any case, they did not arrive empty-hearted or empty-handed. Filled with joy, they brought thoughtful and significant gifts, worthy of a King, a Priest, and a Savior. Gold represented royalty. Frankincense was for worship. Myrrh was precious, and was often used to embalm the dead. These grown, dignified scholars fell on their faces in the presence of the little boy who was the King of Kings and honored His birthday the right way. In so many ways, the Magi model the best Christmas celebrations in all of history.

Practical Recommendations
With this in mind, let's not be like those attending the party for Jessie. Let's emulate the Magi. Here are four recommendations:

Remember it is Someone's Birthday
Don't let gifts, mistletoe, jingle bells, Rudolph, Frosty and Santa draw you away from the purpose of it all. Stay focused with laser precision on the purpose of this Christ mass – His worship.

Remember Whose Birthday It Is
While Christmas is as good a time as any to express your love for friends and family by giving gifts of thoughtful appreciation, we must focus our best and primary giving on the One whose birthday we celebrate. I often challenge people not to give more to others than you give, over and above, to the Christ of Christmas. He is worthy.

Remember What He Wants for His Birthday
We've all felt the frustration of not knowing what gift to buy for someone we care about. So what do we give Christ, the owner of all things? The Bible is clear as to what he wants. He wants our hearts, our worship and our undivided love. Our sacrificial giving should also be consistent with the focus of Christ's affection. The Bible says, "Christ also loved the church and gave Himself for her." The church is described as His very "body." Let your best and biggest gifts to Him be offered to the cause and the people He loves – His church and its mission in this world.

Remember to Give Gifts Fitting for a King
We don't celebrate a season. We celebrate a King. If I were invited to the White House and asked to bring a gift to the President, I would give a lot of care to the selection and presentation of that gift. I would want my thoughtfulness and sacrifice to be fitting of the recipient.

Yet how subordinate the President really is at the feet of King Jesus
This Christmas, let your giving to the Lord be a real act of thoughtful,
sacrificial worship. Let your celebration declare, "Happy Birthday King
Jesus! You are worthy!"

Easter: Feelings or Facts?

As a child, Easter represented new clothes, bunnies, baskets, colored eggs, family meals and a crowded church service. Today, nostalgia often accompanies my memory of how Easter used to be, because it just doesn't feel the same anymore.

I am so thankful that Easter is not about feelings. It's not about eggs or candy. It's not even about family. It is about some glorious facts that must remain as our focus of this celebration. When I remember these truths, something better than nostalgic emotion occurs in my heart. Reassuring hope, joy and peace lift my spirit when I consider the following:

FACT: Because He is risen, I can know that I am saved for eternity. "That if you confess with your mouth the Lord Jesus and believe in your heart that God has raised Him from the dead, you will be saved" Romans 10:9.

FACT: The risen Christ lives in my heart by His Spirit and brings new definition and power to my daily existence.

"But if the Spirit of Him who raised Jesus from the dead dwells in you, He who raised Christ from the dead will also give life to your mortal bodies through His Spirit who dwells in you" Romans 8:11.

FACT: The risen Christ is now the "love of my life," and by His power I can live a significant and fruitful existence.

"Therefore, my brethren, you also have become dead to the law through the body of Christ, that you may be married to another — to Him who was raised from the dead, that we should bear fruit to God" Romans 7:4.

FACT: Because He is risen I am fully alive, seated with Christ and a recipient of the present and eternal riches of His grace.

"But God, who is rich in mercy, because of His great love with which He loved us, even when we were dead in trespasses, made us alive together with Christ (by grace you have been saved), and raised us up together, and made us sit together in the heavenly places in Christ Jesus, that in the ages to come He might show the exceeding riches of His grace in His kindness toward us in Christ Jesus" Ephesians 2:4-7.

FACT: Because He is risen, I can live a life that transcends the temporal and fleeting issues of this life as well as maintain an eternal perspective.

"If then you were raised with Christ, seek those things which are above, where Christ is, sitting at the right hand of God. Set your mind on things above, not on things on the earth" Colossians 3:1-2.

FACT: His resurrection assures me of victory over sin and death and makes my life worth living!

"For this corruptible must put on incorruption, and this mortal must put on immortality. So when this corruptible has put on incorruption, and this mortal has put on immortality, then shall be brought to pass the saying that is written: "Death is swallowed up in victory. O Death, where is your sting? O Hades, where is your victory? The sting of death is sin, and the strength of sin is the law. But thanks be to God, who gives us the victory through our Lord Jesus Christ. Therefore, my beloved brethren, be steadfast, immovable, always abounding in the work of the Lord, knowing that your labor is not in vain in the Lord" 1 Corinthians 15:53-58.

Fact trumps feeling. Let your heart rejoice!

The Prayer of a Godly Mother

Not long ago our family celebrated the life of Vivian Brewer. She went to glory peacefully and eagerly. Great is her reward.

Vivian was my mother-in-law; she gave me the treasure of my wife, Rosemary. She served as a pastor's wife for over sixty years and was probably the most godly woman I have ever known. Several years ago, after her first stroke, she wrote a letter to God. None of us knew about it until it was discovered just days before her death.

The letter was read at her memorial service, and it really represents what we all knew to be true about her. I want to share Vivian's letter with you. I pray it will inspire your heart to seek the Lord and finish well for Christ's glory – even as Vivian did when she stepped into the portals of heaven.

Letter to God

Lord, I'm yours! I want only your will in my life.
I realize I'm not here on earth to do my own thing,
or seek my own fulfillment, or my own glory.
I'm not here to indulge my desires or to increase my
own possessions.
I'm not here to impress people – to be popular or
important,
or to promote myself.
I'm here to please YOU!!
I learned a long time ago to follow Job 13:15
"Though he slay me, yet will I trust him."
I offer myself to you, for you alone are worthy.
I'm yours by creation – all that I am I owe to you!
I receive from you every day – life and breath and all
things. I'm yours!
You bought me and paid the price of your dear son's
blood.
You alone (Father, Son & Spirit) are worthy.
You, my Father, gave to me the Lord Jesus, who gave
Himself for me,
Shed His blood for me, and sent me the empowering of
the Holy Spirit.
I give you my rebellion, which resists your will and
tells me I can do all things in my own power.
I give you my fears, which tell me I'll never be able to
do your will in some areas of my life.
Energize me, oh God, create in me the power and the
desire to do your will.
I give you my body (what there is left of it!) –
my entire inner being, my mind, my emotional life, my
will; my marriage, my children, my grandchildren,
and my great grandchildren; my abilities and gifts,
my strengths and my weaknesses, my heart, my health
(such as it is), my status, my possessions, my past, pres-
ent and future, and when, where, and how I'll go home
to Heaven.

I'm here to love you, obey you, and glorify you!
Oh, Jesus, may I be a joy to you!

Vivian Brewer

P.S. I praise you that you are sovereign!
With you nothing is accidental or incidental.
With you nothing is wasted.
You, Lord, in your power are the breath of life – and all destiny is yours.
You show your love back to me with others looking on.
Thank you that I can move into the future;
for whatever lies ahead, You hold the future.
You will always be with me – even in my old age – and forever!!

True Christmas Worship

One Christmas Day the Blake family was caught up in many of the typical trappings of the season. Things were not going so well. Dad was at his wits end with the malfunctioning tree lights that would not stay on. Mom was in the kitchen sobbing after burning the Christmas casserole. Twin brothers Josh and Jared were in their room screaming as they argued over the new controller for the video games. Older sister Aubrey was in her room pouting because she was not allowed to go to her boyfriend's house for the day.

Witnessing all of this, 4 year old Amber slipped into her bedroom. Kneeling by her bed she earnestly prayed, "Dear God, forgive us our Christmases as we forgive those who Christmas against us."

Like the Blake family, we can easily miss the point of the Christmas season. The value of the family is often eclipsed by the frenzy. Giving is overshadowed by greed. A silent night is drowned out by shopping. Worship is replaced by work, worry and weariness.

Wise Men Really Do Still Seek Him

This Christmas let's revisit the mysterious characters known as the Magi. They can inspire our true worship. As we seek to have Christ-honoring and spiritually meaningful Christmas, we can learn much from these Christ-seekers from the East.

Without too much speculation or detail, it is important to note a few facts about the Magi. These men were students of astrology and astronomy, probably from Persia (modern-day Iran). There is no evidence that there were only three, just that they brought three gifts. They were not from the Orient, nor were they kings. They likely rode on Arabian steeds rather than camels, as is traditionally depicted.

They were likely aware of Balaam's prophecy of the star out of Jacob (Numbers 24:17). We know that the Jews expected a star as a sign of the birth of the Messiah. Somehow, in God's providence these Magi were aware and eager to understand more.

The Magi's example of real worship is notable. I hope it will help you cut through all the clutter of Christmas in order to come back to the heart of worship. We see six characteristics that show us what it means to worship well at Christmas.

Six Keys to Experience True Christmas Worship (Matthew 2:1-11)

Acknowledgement (v. 2)

The account of the Magi's worship journey begins with these words, "Now after Jesus was born in Bethlehem of Judea in the days of Herod the king, behold, wise men from the East came to Jerusalem, saying, 'Where is He who has been born King of the Jews? For we have seen His star in the East...'"

Authentic celebrations of Christmas can only occur when we first acknowledge the identity and character of the Centerpiece of the season. The wise men had been shown by God that the one they sought was not just another religious leader or political figure. He was the King of the Jews, spoken of in prophecy and anticipated by the faithful.

A.W. Tozer wrote , "The essence of idolatry is the entertainment of thoughts about God that are unworthy of Him." Real Christmas worship involves a clear and accurate appreciation for who Christ is. As Warren Wiersbe said, "I am not worshipping Him because of what He will do for me, but because of what He is to me." Worship begins by acknowledging Jesus for who He really is.

The prophet Isaiah spoke of this anticipated King, "For a child will be born to us, a son will be given to us; And the government will rest on His shoulders; And His name will be called Wonderful Counselor, Mighty God, Eternal Father, Prince of Peace. There will be no end to the increase of His government or of peace, on the throne of David and over his kingdom, to establish it and to uphold it with justice and righteousness From then on and forevermore. The zeal of the LORD of hosts will accomplish this." (Isaiah 9:6-7)

Nathanael, the prospective disciple, acknowledged the identity of the King when he said to Jesus, "Rabbi, You are the Son of God; You are the King of Israel" (John 1:49). When He stood before Pilate at His trial Christ testified, "You say correctly that I am a king. For this I have been born, and for this I have come into the world, to testify to the truth. Everyone who is of the truth hears My voice"(John 18:37). Someday in eternity, we will stand before this One who came as a baby on that Christmas night. His identity will be indisputable, "And on His robe and on His thigh He has a name written, 'KING OF KINGS, AND LORD OF LORDS' " (Revelation 19:16).

Over the years, I have shared some key principles of worship. Three come to mind as we think our need to acknowledge Christ this season:

- Worship involves revelation and response. It is the response of all that I am, to the revelation of all that He is.
- To worship "in spirit" involves possession of, submission to, and illumination by the Spirit of God. I cannot worship

effectively apart from the absolute control and wisdom of the Holy Spirit.

- To worship "in truth" involves the truth of God revealed in creation, Christ and the Scriptures – renewing my mind and received in my heart.

The Magi responded to the revelation given them even though it was somewhat obscure and mysterious. We can't help but feel astonishment as we observe their faith and determination to find and worship the young King.

This Christmas, thank the Lord for the full and glorious revelation you have received in His word, His son and the beauty of His world. Worship Him in spirit and in truth, as His indwelling Spirit helps you to acknowledged Christ the Lord in this season of celebration.

Attentiveness (v. 2)

These men were accustomed to gazing at the stars. Yet, they were able to recognize this unique star that would direct them to the Christ child. The passage tells us, "For we have seen His star in the East." Among a countless array of stars in the sky, they were aware that they had seen "His star."

Every Christmas we face the challenge of missing the moment of worship because there are so very many distractions that dull our sensitivity to the central message of Christ. Myriads of lights, commercials, traffic jams and activities can keep us from paying attention to His person and message.

Another principle of worship tells us the enemies of true worship are ignorance, idolatry, impurity, and insincerity.

This Christmas, don't let the confusion of the busy season, the attraction of materialism, the temptations of your heart or the mere religious activities distract you from paying full attention to the one who is worthy of your undivided attention and worship.

Action (v. 2)

Three other principles I've taught over the years are:

- Worship is giving, not receiving. The question is not, "What did I get out of the service?" but "What did God receive from me?"
- Worship is participative, not passive. Worship is a verb, and by definition involves bowing down in order to attribute worth to God.
- Worship involves attitude and action. It is experienced in my innermost being; but, to be sincere, worship must result in acts of sacrificial obedience.

Notice the words of the Magi, ". . . and (we) have come to worship Him." Having seen the star, these wise men were not content to worship from afar. They were determined to make the long trek to find the child. Their worship was more than acknowledgment and attentiveness – but resulted in sacrificial action. For them, it required the thoughtful preparation of gifts, the sacrifice of many days of travel and the inconvenience of rearranging their lives and schedules.

What thoughtful, sacrificial and determined acts of worship will we engage in this Christmas? The New Testament tells us, "Therefore I urge you, brethren, by the mercies of God, to present your bodies a living and holy sacrifice, acceptable to God, which is your spiritual service of worship" Romans 12:1. May the spirit of giving start with our worship of the King as we act in sincere adoration of Him.

Anticipation (vv. 9 & 10)

The passage tells us of the trap Herod was trying to set. After consulting with his advisors about the prophecies of the Messiah, and His future birth in Bethlehem, Herod told the Magi to go find the child. His intention was to use the Magi in order to locate and destroy this "king" who threatened Herod's rule. As we know, God later warned the Magi to avoid Herod's trap and go home by a different route.

After this initial interchange with Herod, the Bible says, "When they heard the king, they departed; and behold, the star which they had seen in the East went before them, till it came and stood over where the young Child was. When they saw the star, they rejoiced with exceedingly great joy."

God now directed these Magi in a very direct and supernatural way, with a stellar manifestation of His glory. The Magi rejoiced with inexpressible, abounding joy – not because of the star, but because of where the star would take them. Their joy was centered in the privilege of worshiping this young King.

A.W. Tozer said, "We are called to an everlasting preoccupation with God." This constant preoccupation is one of great anticipation and joy, knowing how worthy our King is and how "worth it" it is to experience His person and presence.

I've often said "My private expression of worship on Monday through Saturday will determine the fullness of my experience of congregational worship on Sunday."

Psalm 122:1 says, "I was glad when they said to me, 'Let us go to the house of the LORD.' " In Psalm 84:1–2 we read, "How lovely are Your dwelling places, O LORD of hosts! My soul longed and even yearned for the courts of the LORD; My heart and my flesh sing for joy to the living God."

May God give us a consistent anticipation for the joy of daily worship, leading to great rejoicing in our corporate worship – especially at the Christmas season.

Abandonment (v. 11)

Notice this profound commentary: " And when they had come into the house, they saw the young Child with Mary His mother, and fell down and worshiped Him." What a powerful picture of true worship. These grown, dignified and respected men see the young Jesus with his mother. In humble and utter abandonment, they fall on their faces in worship.

Consider this principle of worship:

> *Worship is vertical, not horizontal. God is the audience. I am the performer, invited by His grace to offer a solo to Him. Everyone else is my back-up choir. My goal is not to appease any human on-lookers but to bring pleasure to an audience of one, Him.*

We all can relate to the temptation of worrying more about our dignity than His worthiness when we are in worship. We are often more conscious about the opinions of on lookers than the call of the Savior to praise Him in complete freedom and sincerity.

The Bible compels us abandon our souls and bodies to Him. Come, let us worship and bow down, Let us kneel before the LORD our Maker. (Psalm 95:6). Revelation gives us a glimpse of our worship in Heaven. Surrounded by myriads and myriads of angels we will declare His worth with loud and unrestrained voice. In this futuristic biblical account it says, " the elders fell down and worshiped" (Revelation 5:11-14).

May our worship be so Christ-focuses and unrestrained this Christmas season that we too will honor Him in sweet and sincere abandon.

Adoration (v. 11)

In the familiar narrative, we are told, "And when they had opened their treasures, they presented gifts to Him: gold, frankincense, and myrrh."

We've heard of the beautiful symbolism of these gifts. Gold was a gift for royalty. Christ is the King of the Jews and King of Kings. Frankincense was an expensive fragrance used in worship. This symbolizes Christ's deity. Myrrh seemed a strange gift for a newborn king as it was most commonly used for embalming the dead. Perhaps God led these Magi even in the selection of their gifts as this particular item pointed to his sacrificial death as Savior and Redeemer of the world.

This Christmas we should give our first and best gifts to the "guest of honor" at the birthday celebration. Will these gifts be thoughtful, sacrificial and worthy of Christ?

King David said, " '. . .I will not offer burnt offerings to the LORD my God which cost me nothing'. So David bought the threshing floor and the oxen for fifty shekels of silver" (2 Samuel 24:24). In that same spirit, Paul reminds us "Each one must do just as he has purposed in his heart, not grudgingly or under compulsion, for God loves a cheerful giver. And God is able to make all grace abound to you, so that always having all sufficiency in everything, you may have an abundance for every good deed" (2 Corinthians 9:7-8).

Oh Come Let Us Adore Him!

Let's allow the revelation of all He is to evoke a response of all we are –in true Christmas worship.

William Temple, Archbishop of Canterbury in the mid-20th century said, "To worship is to quicken the conscience by the Holiness of God, to feed the mind with the truth of God, to purge the imagination by the beauty of God, to open the heart to the love of God and devote the will to the purpose of God."

Oh Lord, let this be the nature of our worship this Christmas – for our good, and Your glory!

Notes

1. Brennan Manning, Ruthless Trust (New York: Doubleday, 2000), 5.

2. Jadon Lavik, Meatn to Be from the album Life on the Inside (Seattle: BEC Recordings, 2006).

3. AW Tozer, Of God and Men (Camp Hill, PA: Christian Publications, 1995) 74.

4. John Donne, Devotions Upon Emergent Occasions, Meditation XVII (New York: Cosimo Publishers, 2007) 108.

5. Arthur Helps, as quoted at http://famouspoetsandpoems.com/thematic_quotes/strength_quotes.html

6. Mother Theresa of Avila, as quoted at http://www.quotesea.com/Quotes.aspx?about=Endurance

7. Watchman Nee, The Normal Christian Life (Fort Washington, PA: Christians Literature Crusade, 1973)

8. Cindy Adams, Maher's New Movie to Stir Religious Pot (New York: NewYorkPost.com, February 28, 2008)

9. Ernest Hemmingway, The Complete Short Stories of Earnest Hemmingway (New York: Simon & Schuster, 1998) p. 29

10. Phil Ryken, The Prayer of Our Lord (Wheaton, IL: Crossway, 2002) p. 55

11. Martin Lloyd Jones as quote on The Quoteable Christian (www.pietyhilldesign.com/gcq/quotepages/forgiveness.html)

12. Ken Sande, The Peacemaker (Grand Rapids: Baker, 2004), 217

13. Henry Ward Beecher as quoted on www.brainyquote.com

14. Jon Meacham, The End of Christian America (New York: Newsweek, Newsweek.com, April 12, 2009)

15. Michael Spencer, The Coming Evangelical Collapse (Boston: Christian Science Monitor, CSMonitor.com, March 10, 2008)

16. Barak Obama, as quoted on Media Matters for America (http://mediamatters.org/research/200904090033)

17. Dogwood, After the Flood Before the Fire (Nashville: Lamb and Lion Recored, 1975)

18. AW Tozer, The root of the Righteous (Camp Hill, PA: Winsgpread Publishers, 2004) 31.

19. Ibid, 32.

20. Ibid, 34.

21. Ibid, 36.

22. Jonathan Edwards, in Archie Parish and R.C. Sproul, The Spirit of Revival (Wheaton, Il: Crossway, 2000), 93.

23. Charles Haddon Spurgeon, Lectures to My Students (Charleston, S.C.: Bibliolife, 2009) 47.

24. J. Oswald Sanders, Spirtiual Leadership (Chicago: Moody Press, 1994) 86.

25. Arthur G. Bennet, Valley of Vision (Carlisle, PA: Banner of Truth, 2003), 2.